MW01295476

KAYAK EASTERN CONNECTICUT

70 EASTERN CT PADDLING DESTINATIONS

LOU RACINE

Author of
DOG PADDLING WITH TINY:
A Guide To Kayaking With a Dog

Copyright © 2016 Lou Racine

ISBN-13: 978-1523447923

ISBN-10: 1523447923

Indian Leap page 105

To April, Barbara, Denise, and Yvonne

My greatest desire is to inspire others as much as you have inspired me! Thank you!

Paddle on,

Special Thanks

Special thank you to Cecil for being the wonderfully thoughtful, caring, and supportive person behind my adventures and my writing. Cec, because of you, my life is a non-stop adventure! -- and we all know how much I love a good adventure!

-- From my heart, thank you.

ACKNOWLEDGEMENTS

The safety tips presented in this book have been included in memory of a young potential paddler lost too soon.

Last summer, a teen died while attempting to kayak on the potentially dangerous Shetucket River. This tragic accident hit me hard because I had lost my own 18 year old son in a car accident. There have been significant efforts to help teens drive more safely, and as a result, I have felt as if I couldn't significantly add to that effort.

However, after this tragic kayaking accident on the Shetucket River, I realized that there are potentially countless opportunities for writers and paddlers, such as myself, to inform and possibly help to prevent such tragedies from occurring again. Unlike teen driving, informing teens about the hazards surrounding this increasingly popular sport has been minimal.

Potential paddlers who are new to the sport may not recognize the dangers more easily identified by more seasoned paddlers. As a result, they may put their lives, and possibly the lives of others, in danger without realizing the gamble they have under taken. For these reasons, I have included paddling safety tips and placed significant effort on thoroughly outlining the potential hazards and risks that are known to me, and that I have witnessed, while paddling the sites presented in this book. For the more seasoned paddlers who may think that this precautionary information is unnecessary, thank you for understanding its purpose.

Kayaking CT with Lou is currently seeking to engage in collaborative efforts to inform and teach teens and children about the risks involved in kayaking, while at the same time, encouraging them to safely engage in this sport. If you would like to help, have advice or ideas, or you wish to donate supplies, time, or money, feel free to contact Lou at KayakingCTwithLou@paddlingCT.com. *(Please no solicitation).*

INTRODUCTION

Do you find yourself struggling to squeeze kayaking into your schedule? Are you frustrated with a lack of available information regarding the sites you are thinking about paddling? Have you ever said, "Wow, I never knew that site existed? Well, this book will help solve these issues and more!

Fuel your sense of adventure with Lou's paddling guide book for Eastern Connecticut! This book contains the expected, the unexpected, and more, including coastal access, rivers, lakes, islands, ponds, and even river camping in Eastern Connecticut! Each entry includes a brief description, launch info, date last paddled, and a site review as experienced by the author. Site information will also include information regarding hiking, camping, and other available activities when appropriate. For your convenience, this book is presented in alphabetical order, indexed alphabetically and by town, and launch and basic information appear first for each entry.

Lou won't try to sell you on every site either. Paddlers will receive an honest opinion and factual review of each site including boat launch information so that paddlers can decide which sites best fit their individual needs! After all, that's what a guide book should be all about; it should never be about convincing readers to paddle every site in the state!

This book exists to save you time, money, and frustration! Let Lou show you around these Eastern Connecticut paddling destinations so paddlers can spend their time and money on the water having fun!

Featured paddling site:

Cover Photo. Photo page 10.

LIEUTENANT RIVER TO GREAT ISLAND

CONNECTICUT RIVER BY-PASS

LYME, CT

This trip is interesting from a birding perspective and it also has a few points of interest, including the Great Island Estuary (page 79), the lighthouse *(cover photo)*, and the draw bridge *(See photo page 10)*.

The Connecticut River by-pass paddle from the Lieutenant River to the back side of Marvin Island and on to the Great Island launch is an awesome birding paddle; but, also a way to avoid paddling against the tide on the Connecticut River for a nice round trip paddle, starting and ending at either of the two launches involved. There are a few ways to use this paddle pass-through behind Marvin Island and Great Island. Paddlers can paddle with the tide up or down that section of the Connecticut River and then form a loop by going down or up the back passage behind the two Islands, and thereby avoid paddling against the tide on the Connecticut River. Paddlers could also paddle both ways on the back passage behind Marvin Island and Great Island and avoid paddling on the Connecticut River all together, starting at one launch and ending at the other, or by returning to the same launch.

I recommend ending at the Great Island Launch over the Lieutenant River Launch because paddlers will have more options if they find they have additional time. For example, paddlers could go up the Black Hall River (short distance at low tide) or paddle around Great Island and stop at one of the sandy beaches (tide can affect access). The Great

Island boat launch is near the mouth of the Connecticut River and also provides coastal access to the sound. Low tide can affect access to some areas involved in this back passage. *(Great Island photo page 80)*

TYPE: Tidal River, Birding

LAUNCH INFO:

The Great Island launch is located at 99 Smith Neck Road (off Rte 156), in Old Lyme, CT and is 500' from Great Island. Nice parking area, turning area, and ramp. In addition to close and almost immediate access to the Great Island Wildlife Preserve, this launch also provides an access point for Long Island Sound, places like the Black Hall River, and the back entrance to the Lieutenant River discussed above.

The Lieutenant River launch is located by a bridge on Route 156 (Shore Road) near Ferry Road in Old Lyme. Turn right from the stop sign at Ferry Road and the launch will be on the left after the bridge on Route 156.

LAST PADDLED: 9/9/15

OUR EXPERIENCES:

On our most recent paddle, we paddled left from the Great Island Launch to the mouth of the Connecticut River, then across the Connecticut River to the Light House, where we ate lunch and watched boats on the less populated beach to the north *(cover photo)*. When high tide started to really kick in, we decided to ride the current up to the draw bridge *(photo page 10)*. The tide-assist was great fun and required very little paddling.

We didn't want to paddle back against that strong current so we ducked into the mouth of the Lieutenant River *(right side of the draw bridge when paddling up river)*, then took the first right and meandered our way down to the back side of Marvin Island and on to the back side of Great Island, enjoying a wide variety of birds along the way. This back way to the Great Island Launch is a very nice birding experience!

If paddlers enter the mouth of the Lieutenant River to do this (as we did), and they arrive at the Lieutenant River Launch at the bridge, then they've gone too far. A GPS could assist paddlers in finding this access point, as well as, assist paddlers as they meander through the channels, peninsulas, grasses, and mini islands involved in this paddle pass-through.

Earlier this season, I paddled around Great Island and enjoyed watching osprey feeding their young at the many nesting platforms located on, and in the area of, Great Island. We also got out and spent time on the long stretch of beach located on the Connecticut River side of Great Island. Tide will affect beach access. Paddlers will likely see gulls and pipers, as we did, on the Connecticut River side of the island as well.

Due to the immediate access to the Sound, I recommend using a sea kayak--especially if there is wind or other conditions that would increase waves and current. *Paddle at your own risk and discretion; only you can determine what is, or is not, safe and appropriate for you and your level of experience and condition.*

Riding the tide up the Connecticut River from the lighthouse..
See featured site on page 7 & lighthouse cover image.

DISCLAIMER

Paddle at your own risk and discretion; only you can determine what is, or is not, safe and appropriate for you and your level of experience and condition. It is your responsibility to determine the legality, suitability, and safety of paddling at the destinations and paddling routes in this book. Read all applicable signs at the launch sites and be aware of boating regulations for each specific area before paddling. The author assumes no liability for accidents happening to, and/or injuries and/or damages sustained by readers and/or others who engage in the activities in this book.

This book contains facts and also the opinions of the author who has paddled at each paddling destination in this book, unless otherwise stated. The opinions expressed in this book are those of the author and may not represent the opinion of others who may be mentioned in this book. It is a reference book for informational purposes only and should not be the sole source of information for paddling the sites presented in this book.

Immature eagle looking out over the Quinebaug River
near Butts Bridge in Canterbury, CT.
(*See page 51*)

ALVIA CHASE RESERVOIR

EAST KILLINGLY, CT

Alvia Chase Reservoir is one of the smallest of the five East Killingly reservoirs clustered together in North Eastern Connecticut. However, paddlers should not let the initial view fool them into thinking this pond is tiny. While it is small, Alvia Chase Reservoir continues under the Route 101 bridge, and is bigger than it appears at first glance.

I wouldn't recommend a trip out there just to paddle on Alvia Chase Reservoir; however, if paddling in the area, it might be worth a peek. There are four other reservoirs in the immediate area: Middle Reservoir across the street, Killingly Pond and Eddy Pray Reservoirs a couple minutes up the road (from Route 101), and The Bog on nearby Bear Hill Road. Eddy Pray can be difficult to find *(See page 61)*.

TYPE: Reservoir/Pond

LAUNCH INFO:

Alvia Chase Reservoir is located on Pond Road off Route 101 in East Killingly, CT; Alvia Chase Reservoir will be on the right and Middle Reservoir on the left. There are several pull-off parking areas on both sides of the road. The launch area for Alvia Chase Reservoir is to the right of the pond facing it. Although the launch is rustic, it's typically easy to enter and exit the water there.

LAST PADDLED: 7/30/14

OUR EXPERIENCES:

Our last paddle at this location, as is usually the case, occurred because we were in the area paddling one of the other Killingly Reservoirs earlier in the day. There was a little daylight left, and we weren't ready to call it a day yet, so we launched on Alvia Chase Reservoir.

We walked our hands along the under-side of the Route 101 bridge and guided our kayaks to the other side where we did some kayak birding. We were rewarded with what I believe to have been a Warbler sighting. There are more lily pads and vegetation in the area past the bridge; but, nothing that hinders paddling.

Middle Reservoir is across the street from Alvia Chase Reservoir and is a better birding location; however, it can be an arduous paddle due to the over growth of vegetation and the number of mosquitoes during some times of the year. *See Middle Reservoir page 127.*

I spent many evenings fishing and paddling here, and at the other four reservoirs, when I was a kid.

NOTES:

AMOS LAKE

PRESTON, CT

Amos Lake is 113 acres and about 1/3 of it is heavily populated. Unless fishing, I would not recommend kayaking on Amos Lake. I casually paddled around it in about an hour and the only interesting thing I saw was a single cormorant.

TYPE: Lake

LAUNCH INFO:

The boat launch is located on Route 164 in Preston, CT. Watch for boat signs. It has a nice launch and parking area.

LAST PADDLED: SUMMER 2014

OUR EXPERIENCES:

I was greatly unimpressed with this location from a recreational paddler's perspective. It has a nice launch; however, paddling this lake did not hold my interest even a little bit. I paddled alone on Amos Lake with my dog on a weekday, but, as I was leaving (about 6pm), two motor boats arrived and were being unloaded, and I heard another start up somewhere across the lake. Judging by the number of motor boats I saw docked and the two that arrived as I was leaving, makes me believe that this pond is probably an active place on the weekends.

I would suggest nearby Avery Pond to paddlers who are interested in bird watching and who are already in the immediate area. Avery Pond is a <u>tiny</u> pond; but, I've seen several interesting birds on it. My dog, and I, spent as much time on the much smaller Avery Pond watching the different birds as I did kayaking on Amos Lake and enjoyed bird watching on Avery Pond more! *(See Avery Pond. Page 25)*

NOTES:

ASHLAND POND:
PACHAUG RIVER

JEWETT CITY, CT

The Pachaug "River" is actually a collection of dammed ponds with little tail-like stretches of "river" attached to them. Unlike the local Quinebaug River, this river cannot be paddled for long uninterrupted distances due to the dams separating the ponds from other portions of the river. For this reason, these different sections of the Pachaug River will be presented under the pond to which the little river tail is attached.

Paddling left from the informal Norman Road launch will bring paddlers into Ashland Pond; paddling right will start their journey up river towards the Hopeville Pond falls. It is for the most part, a meandering river with only a few areas that need to be portaged or wiggled through. The current does increase as paddlers approach the falls; however, it is possible to paddle up river and reach the falls early in the season before water levels recede later on *(See our experiences below)*.

Ashland Pond is a mixture, ranging from clear water to areas that are so weedy that it can inhibit paddling. For the most part, it is open and easily paddled. It is lightly populated, and more so on the right side than the left when facing the pond from the Norman Road Bridge. There is a small cemetery to the left: however, other than that, the left side is for the most part wooded shoreline. Unless fishing, I'd head up river, returning to the pond if time remained after the river quest.

TYPE: Pond, Pachaug River Access

LAUNCH INFO:

There is an unofficial boat launch area on both sides of the Norman Road bridge in Jewett City, CT. The right side is cleared better, has a wider launch area, and is adjacent to the informal pull-off parking area. We've put our kayaks in on both sides without issue; although, I recommend the launch adjacent to the parking area.

<u>Note</u>: I have seen adult and immature snakes near, and around, the launch area on a few occasions.

LAST PADDLED: **2015 (4x)**

OUR EXPERIENCES:

I've paddled up river from this boat launch a few times during the 2015 season and paddled around the pond only a couple of times in my life time. The river is truly the main attraction at this site. During one of the few times that I paddled the pond, our timely, yet unplanned, arrival at the far side of Ashland Pond was rewarded with the melodious 5:00 chimes of the local church. It was a nice break from the sound of distant traffic.

Paddling up river from this location is best done early in the season when the water level is high; but, not immediately following spring thaw. When the water level is low, paddlers may not be able to paddle all the way to the falls and back. Lower water level will definitely mean more exposed rocks and tree limbs to shimmy over, squeeze under, or portage around.

As paddlers get closer to the falls, and the current significantly increases, they should see a foot bridge crossing the river in the distance.. At this point, paddlers should start looking for a canal on the right. At the end of the 2015 season, there was a large fallen tree that obscures the entrance to this canal. This canal is typically easier to paddle than the increasing current on the river facing the upcoming falls.

At the end of the canal, paddlers will be facing a water fall. Getting in and out of a kayak at the canal falls can be dangerous! The rocks can be slippery and loose. If paddlers chose to get out and explore, they should do so at their own risk and discretion.

Up over the hill to the left is the foot bridge mentioned earlier. The separate two tiered falls that was causing the current in the main river can be seen from the foot bridge. Crossing the foot bridge and walking up around the falls, paddlers will see Hopeville Pond. Caution, the ground near the pond is sometimes very muddy. *(See Hopeville Pond page 99).*

NOTES:

RIVER PADDLING TIP

Consider putting an **"If Found" sticker** on your kayak or the same information in a prominent place on the kayak. If a paddler's kayak gets away from them and they are not able to retrieve it and it is found on the water, the shoreline, floating against a dam, etc., and this results in a search for the owner, the paddler could be held accountable for the cost of that erroneous search!

In some cases, the Coast Guard provides these stickers free of charge. They can also be purchased online for a minimal fee. The sticker provides the finder of the kayak with the paddler's phone number and an alternate phone number which should be the person who would most likely know where the paddler should be and if the paddler is all right.

Note: Creative paddlers who don't want their phone number exposed to every onlooker as they paddle can cover the phone numbers with something that only blocks the phone numbers without damaging the writing or visually interrupting the overall purpose of the sticker.

ASPINOOK POND: QUINEBAUG RIVER

GRISWOLD, CT

Aspinook Pond is part of the Quinebaug River and located in Griswold, CT. I usually use the Aspinook launch as a take-out for Quinebaug River paddles that begin at more northern locations, such as Butts Bridge, Robert Manship Park/Canterbury Bridge, and the Plainfield Launch.

The opposite end of the pond is dammed. This is a functioning dam and I have, on occasion, experienced some significant drag towards the falls near the buoyed area before the falls. I suggest paddlers stay back away from that area and do not attempt to portage this dam.

Paddlers who have never paddled at this location, may be momentarily awe struck by the size of this pond as they initially paddle into it. However, they will quickly notice that the wooded shoreline is moderately populated and so there is almost always houses, campers, railroad tracks, boats, or someone's back yard within the paddler's view.

This area is sometimes busy with jet skis and motor boats during the peak boating season. For this reason, I usually paddle above the Butts Bridge launch as it is far less populated and there is less motor traffic.

TYPE: River, Pond

LAUNCH INFO:

From the river:

The launch is located within a cove off the upper section of Aspinook Pond and is not visible from the river. Paddlers who are paddling down river, will not see the launch from the river, and in the summer, the cove entrance can be difficult to identify as well. I've paddled past the cove entrance and I know where it is! In the fall and winter months, the cove entrance is more obvious. Paddlers who are not familiar with this launch, and who are using it as a take out point for a summer river paddle from a northern launch, may want to use GPS to locate it, or take a few minutes to paddle out through the cove and mark the cove entrance or pick a landmark that will be familiar when paddling down river later. Please remove any markers when done paddling.

Directions to the launch:

The Aspinook Pond boat launch area is easily accessible, but has only a few spaces for parking vehicles. From Rte 12 in Griswold, CT, take Quinebaug Camp Road, then left onto Arbor Road. Follow Arbor Road almost to the end, watching for a narrow dirt road on the right that leads down to the water *(this may not be obvious in the summer)*. About half way down this dirt access road, visitors will see a sign stating, "Closed at Sunset....." and then the launch site a short distance beyond that sign.

LAST PADDLED: FALL 2015

OUR EXPERIENCES:

Most recently, I paddled around Aspinook Pond with my dog. On other occasions, I have sailed my kayak and done some metal detecting and magnet fishing on this pond.

As I stated earlier, I generally use the launch at this location for a take out point when paddling down from northern areas of the Quinebaug River. Paddling from Canterbury bridge/Robert Manship Park launch *(See page 175)* to this location usually takes us about 3 - 3 ½ hours with a slight spring current; a little longer later in the season when the current isn't as strong. Of course, the amount of time depends upon how much lingering is going on as well. The distance between Butts Bridge and Aspinook Pond would be a very short paddle and one that I would not consider to be worth the effort to set up.

NOTES:

SAFETY TIP FOR WOMEN

Women who are paddling alone or in small groups should not hesitate to phone or text the license plate of a suspicious vehicle to a reliable friend or family member. The paddler may, or may not, choose to be obvious about it based on their current situation. There is no exact answer as to what should be done because each situation is different. Paddlers who feel threatened should immediately contact the police!

Last summer, a friend and I were approached by three men as we were getting into our kayaks at an otherwise vacant launch. The three men asked us leading and unusual questions that caused us to be suspicious. After talking with us, they mulled around by their truck on the other side of the parking area, chatting and pointing.

I opened a text window on my phone and then pretended to have difficulty making out the license plate as I entered the info into my phone. I did this so that it would be very obvious that the plate was what I was looking at, and I actually texted the license plate and related info to my boyfriend, and then snapped a couple of photos of the truck with them near it. I also took a photo of a car that was parked near the launch (including its license plate) just in case something came of this situation; the owner might have seen something earlier or might see something later that could be helpful should a situation arise from this encounter.

One of the men yelled over, asking if I was texting the cops. I didn't answer and we quickly paddled off. They drove off just as quickly and we never saw them again.

NOTE: I utilize the Drop Box APP so photos go immediately to my computer. If my phone were taken from me, I dropped it in the water, or it was otherwise damaged during a scuffle, the photos would be preserved on my computer at home.

AVERY POND

PRESTON, CT

Avery Pond is located in Preston CT and is only **36 acres**; so paddlers won't be doing a lot of paddling; however, this pond has something to offer to those paddlers who are into **BIRD WATCHING** and also interested in hanging out on the water. Being in a kayak at this location allows birders to get very close to the birds.

TYPE: Small Pond, Bird Watching

LAUNCH INFO:

The launch for this site was quite unexpected! It's a beautiful launch that one might expect to see at a larger lake, not at a tiny pond. There is ample parking and a solid gently sloping launch. The boat launch area for Avery Pond is located on Lynn Drive off Route 164 in Preston, CT. There is a boat launch sign on Route 164 at the intersection of Lynn Road.

LAST PADDLED: 7/10/14

OUR EXPERIENCES:

Our dog, Tiny, and I arrived on a weekday at about 6 pm. Within minutes of being on the water, a large heron flew from the bushes and nearly knocked my dog off the deck of my kayak! I'm sure, it's as close to a heron as my dog ever wants to be again! LOL! It caught me totally off guard because I was watching the ducks lazily floating around us without concern.

I watched a pair of cormorants swimming, diving, and staying under for almost a minute each time and a large brown bird with a lighter underbelly that I could not identify in the evening light. The large bird skimmed across the water touching the water every few feet, circling around and doing it again and again, finally perching high up in a tree when it realized we were close by. After a while, it returned to its previous task of repeatedly skimming across the water when it seemed to realize we were only watchers and not to be feared. I saw several smaller birds of interest as well. For such a small area of water, there were a lot of birds and the kayak allowed us to get very close to them.

We encountered people fishing from the launch on one occasion.

NOTES:

BEACH POND

VOLUNTOWN, CT

This almost 400 acre pond is at the source of the Pachaug River; however, unlike the other ponds associated with the Pachaug River, Beach Pond does not have a paddleable tail like stretch of river attached to it.

It can be surprisingly busy even on weekday afternoons. During the boating season, jet skiers, motor boats, water skiers, canoes and kayaks, are usually a constant on the water in the afternoon. Most of the houses are on the side that is opposite the boat ramp and most of the rocky inlet type cove areas are on the launch side of the pond.

It is sometimes possible to squeeze under the bridge to the back of the pond *(left of the launch);* however, waves from boats and wind can make this extremely dangerous *(See our experiences below)*. Paddlers who attempt this, do so at your own risk and discretion.

TYPE: Lake

LAUNCH INFO:

Beach Pond has a nice tarred entry, parking area, and a cement boat launch. The launch is located at 205 North Shore Road in Voluntown, CT

LAST PADDLED: 7/23/14

OUR EXPERIENCES:

I had my dog with me; however, I would not bring him to this location again, nor would I recommend bringing a dog to paddle at this location due to the constant motor traffic and water skiing. My dog was never alarmed; however, he was never as restful as he generally is when kayaking.

The under-populated side of the pond was interesting, but overall this is not a pond that I would recommend for recreational kayaking or canoeing when there are so many other ponds and lakes in the area. We did see several fishermen in the little inlets and along the edges of the pond so fishing might be an option.

We paddled around the entire pond, but did not squeeze under the bridge at the far end. I didn't want to duck so low, and for that distance, with my dog on board. Passing under that bridge might look inviting; however, paddlers must strongly consider the water level, boat traffic, and the potential for boat traffic, when deciding the outcome of this idea. It is possible to get to the other side and not be able to come back due to waves from boat traffic slapping water up towards the under side of the bridge. It is possible to be under the bridge and get sloshed into the bridge from boat waves. Going under this bridge is a gamble at best, and has the potential to be very dangerous within the right set of circumstances. If you choose to paddle under the bridge, do so at your own risk and discretion.

When darkness started to creep in everyone packed up and went home. It happened so fast that my friend and I looked at each other and chuckled because suddenly it was quiet, the previously wavy water was like glass, and we were seemingly alone! We enjoyed the quieter evening and night hours we spent on the pond more than the time spent on it in daylight.

BEACHDALE POND:
PACHAUG RIVER

VOLUNTOWN, CT

Do not confuse Beachdale Pond with Beach Pond. Both are in the same area.

The Pachaug "River" is actually a collection of dammed ponds with little tail-like stretches of "river" attached to them. Unlike the local Quinebaug River, this river cannot be paddled for long uninterrupted distances due to the dams separating the ponds from other portions of the river. For this reason, sections of the Pachaug River will be presented with the pond to which the little river tail is attached.

There is more here than 45 acres of pond! Beachdale Pond and the adjoining swamp is a wonderful birding area if paddling alone, or paddling in stealth mode with a very small group! This pond is also part of the Pachaug River and this launch provides access to that as well.

The demarcation for Beachdale Pond and the Pachaug River is the Route 49 Bridge. The pond flows out and to the left and right after passing under the bridge. Under the bridge and to the right *(after the section of pond)* is rustic access to an open swamp which includes tall trees, privacy, and even active beaver lodges *(water level, paddler's level of enthusiasm, and under brush may limit access)*. Paddlers wishing to paddle in the swamp will have to shimmy against the current over a small beaver dam and press their way through grasses and light under brush *(See photo page 32)*. How far one can paddle in the swamp is dependant upon time of year, number of fallen trees and branches, and water level.

Inexperienced paddlers might be fooled into thinking that the water at this location is safe shallow pond water; but, in reality the mud is so deep in some areas that if a paddler were to fall in, getting out of the mud could be very difficult. I have pressed my paddle down into the mud in some areas of the pond and river and sometimes had difficulty pulling the paddle back out! There were areas where the mud level on my extracted paddle was at least 3x deeper than the water above it! Depending upon the time of year, there can be a lot of vegetation in some areas that can get hung up on paddles as well.

Left of the boat launch is the Pachaug River which can be paddled as well; however, it isn't always easy and mosquitoes are often an issue *(See our experiences below)*. This launch also provides access to Beaver City *(Page 33)*.

TYPE: River, Bird Watching, Fishing

LAUNCH INFO:

The boat launch for Beachdale Pond is located near MT Misery Campground on Route 49 (just a short distance from Route 138) in Voluntown, CT. It will be on the right before Mt Misery Campground when arriving from Route 138. There is ample parking and trailer access.

LAST PADDLED: Summer 2015 (3x)

OUR EXPERIENCES:

I would recommend Beachdale Pond and the adjoining swamp to birding and wildlife enthusiasts who can paddle in stealth mode. I've been up close and personal with a variety of birds at this location, sometimes while tucked in some corner, out of sight, eating lunch. On one occasion, while taking a break, a flock of geese crossed so close to my kayak that I could have reached out and touched one!

While paddling on Beachdale Pond, we saw ducks, 4 different herons, geese, and a swan family during our second trip of the season. On our third visit of the season, we came within twelve feet of a swan *(careful swans can be aggressive, especially when nesting or with a nesting partner)*. On the first trip we had more people and didn't see as much. However, our first trip of the season did hold the interest of a child. Her enthusiasm put a permanent smile on my face for the entire time we were out on the water.

When paddling up river, the river becomes more private after passing the campground on the right. I've found that someone regularly cuts away the fallen trees in this part of the river so passage in that respect is usually easy. With fallen trees cut away, I have been able to paddle a significant distance up river, eventually reaching a point where I have to paddle as if paddling a canoe, using only one half of the paddle.

This trek actually becomes a bit eerie due to the silence and the narrowing tunnel of foliage closing in on the pollen and algae covered water. I've literally paddled until I ran out of paddleable water and had to remove my kayak, turn it around on the embankment, and head back. LOL! I have paddled up river to the left of this launch with my dog several times over the years; however, I'm usually taking the right turn to Beaver City *(Page 33)*.

It is interesting to see humming birds in their natural habitat on this portion of the river and not just at backyard feeders and in flower gardens. They seem to like the red flowers. Way up this narrowing river is very isolated and the mosquitoes are usually out in force; so, if choosing this route, bring spray!

NOTES:

Making our way to the swamp from Beachdale Pond
(See page 29)

BEAVER CITY: PACHAUG RIVER

VOLUNTOWN, CT

Many people take advantage of the Beachdale Pond/Pachaug River boat launch (Route 49) near Mt Misery Campground in Voluntown, CT; however, very few people make the trek from this location to the Shetucket Turnpike Bridge and back! One reason for this is that the entrance to this water trail becomes obscured by weeds later in the season, causing kayakers to pass by it without noticing this secondary option. Others see the option; but, turn back at the first beaver dam! The right turn to Beaver City can be found on a map or by using a GPS and paddling is easier before those weeds mature in June.

In addition to using a GPS to find the entrance, I also recommend using a GPS tracker when paddling through this section because there are swamp trails that can easily lead paddlers off course if they don't occasionally check their position. Don't be misled to believe that paddling this waterway is easy because it's not. Be sure to read our experiences below before attempting to paddle this section of the Pachaug River.

TYPE: Rustic River/Swamp, Well seasoned paddlers only

CAUTION:

I don't recommend paddling any part of this location, day or night, unless paddlers are well seasoned river paddlers and have prior and significant experience paddling these conditions, and are using the appropriate equipment, PFD, waterproof lighting, and GPS. Even then, please recognize the possible dangers involved in doing so.

The swamp waterways of this location are like a maze and can confuse even people who are familiar with it, and while the waterways are narrow, they are sometimes deep! At first glance, this section may seem shallow; however, I have lowered my paddle to a depth that covered 3/4 of my paddle in more than one location. Paddlers who get lost should not panic because in reality they are not that far from one end or the other. Paddle at your own risk; only you can determine what is, or is not, safe and appropriate for you and your level of experience and condition.

BTW, there are bats under the Shetucket Turnpike Bridge. I've found them to be harmless if left alone. I only mention them so that paddlers will realize what they are when they fly out! LOL!

LAUNCH INFO:

This trip originates at the Beachdale Pond Boat Launch (Route 49) near MT Misery Campground in Voluntown, CT. Paddle left from the launch and then take the first right *(left at this V will take paddlers to Great Meadow Brook)*. I recommend that paddlers follow a map or GPS to find this right turn and to find their way along this route to the Shetucket Turnpike Bridge and back.

LAST PADDLED: 6/3/15

OUR EXPERIENCES:

Our last paddle to Beaver City, and on to the Shetucket Turnpike Bridge and back, was done by day and night. We paddled ¾ of the way back in daylight, and passed through Beaver City by the cover of night and fog, in the hopes of seeing some beavers as we passed back through Beaver City.

We did this 3.6 mile trip from the Beachdale River launch to the Shetucket Turnpike Bridge falls and back in 4 1/2 hours. We returned after dark; the drifting mist, along with the peaceful sounds of the peepers and bullfrogs, caused us to linger several times. I find this paddle to be an exhilarating and challenging paddle while at the same time it relaxes and unwinds my mind. Going to the gym can't come close to this workout!

This is not a trip for the faint of heart or those who are not in top physical condition! There is one large beaver dam, 2 smaller ones, downed trees (*1 must be portaged and a couple shimmied over*), as well as low hanging branches and other obstacles to be evaluated and dealt with. In one instance during our last paddle, I had to duck low under a branch of a fallen tree, lean heavy to one side, and at the same time, maneuver over another branch from that same tree. Later, I called to wish a relative Happy Birthday while contemplating what to do about being stuck on yet another tree that I had attempted to shimmy over. During our last paddle, we only had to portage 3x; however, one portage meant dragging our kayaks a short distance through the woods.

"Why go?" You ask! If "because it's there" doesn't cut it, beyond the initial beaver dam is a section that we commonly refer to as Beaver City. Paddlers can see all aspects of a beaver's life, from pre-construction to enormous huts, food storage, as well as beaver dams...and if paddlers are quiet and a little bit lucky, they might even see beavers!

NOTE: Theoretically, if one were able to go forward at the falls just past the Shetucket Turnpike Bridge they would eventually arrive at the dam at Beach Pond; however, to do so would mean invading upon private property at the falls. I don't yet know if the river is paddle able beyond the small pond located at these falls and I have no personal knowledge of the small stretch of river between these falls and Beach Pond. This section of river is on our short list to be scouted as potential site for our annual challenge paddle.

RIVER SAFETY TIP

River paddlers should carry a water proof whistle or other loud noise producing item, such as a horn, on their person while paddling rivers. This whistle should be attached to the PFD, secured in a zip pocket, or in some other way that it will be easily accessible in an emergency. A whistle or horn can be heard over the sound of current, motor boats, and falls more easily than the sound of a person yelling. Blowing a whistle is much easier for an exhausted paddler than yelling, and it can be heard from a greater distance.

BEEBE COVE
NOANK, CT

The Beebe Cove launch provides access to Mystic Harbor, Mystic River, and beyond. This can also be a take-out launch for a down river paddle on the Mystic River *(See Mystic River State Boat Launch on page 133)*.

TYPE: Tidal cove with coastal & Mystic Harbor access

LAUNCH INFO:

The Beebe Cove launch is located behind the Noank Recreation Department building on Spicer Avenue in Noank, CT. This is a beautiful launch which includes a traditional launch area and a dock launch which allows paddlers to slip into a sloping area within the dock that stabilizes the kayak while the paddler gets in/out! This public launch is closed at dusk.

Access to Mystic Harbor, Six Penny Island, Mason Island, Ram Island, Mystic River, and beyond can be found by passing under the railroad bridge which is across the cove and slightly to the right of this launch. This can also be a take-out launch for a down river paddle on the Mystic River. *(See Mystic River State Boat Launch on page 133)*.

CAUTION:

Beebe Cove, itself, is a small sheltered tidal area; it is connected to the mouth of the Mystic River and Mystic Harbor by the water flowing under the railroad bridge. The current pushing its way under that bridge can be significant at the onset of high or low tide and during some weather conditions.

After going under that bridge and leaving Beebe Cove, paddlers will see Mason Island ahead and slightly to the left. Paddlers who paddle south of Mason Island could quickly find themselves paddling out into open water; paddling beyond Costello's Crab Shack and that immediate area is open water! Ram Island and Fishers Island are located in that open water. THIS IS NOT A PLACE FOR BEGINNERS!

Only very seasoned river paddlers who are also experienced paddling this type of open water under a variety of conditions should be paddling from this location; all other paddlers should seek assistance from an experienced guide. Weather and conditions can sometimes quickly and unpredictably change paddling conditions here. I strongly recommend using a skirted sea kayak and not a recreational kayak in the water beyond this cove.

LAST PADDLED: Summer 2015 (4x)

OUR EXPERIENCES:

We have paddled from this location to nearby Mason Island and to slightly farther destinations such as Ram Island, Enders Island, and Morgan Point. This is our go-to take-out for down river paddles on the Mystic River because it is the most southern take-out. BTW the ice cream at the shop beside the Mystic River draw bridge is just awesome!

NOTES:

BIGELOW HOLLOW POND

UNION, CT

Bigelow Hollow Pond, Mashapaug Lake, and the smaller Breakneck Pond are all located within Bigelow Hollow State Park in Union, CT. Bigelow Pond is small and primarily a fishing site, and Mashapaug Lake is larger and more of a recreational site. As of the writing of this book, there is a $9/car weekend entrance fee to Bigelow Hollow State Park.

The sign at the Bigelow Hollow Pond boat launch states that pickerel, large and small mouth bass, walleye, brown and rainbow trout, and pumpkin seed reside in Bigelow Hollow Pond.

Don't under-estimate a trip to Bigelow Hollow Park based on this one pond. Please also read the entry for Mashapaug Lake *(Page 121)*. The park itself, which includes Bigelow Pond, Mashapaug Lake, and a third smaller pond located about 1 mile into the woods, also offers hiking, fishing, cross country skiing, swimming, boating, and some nice picnic areas.

TYPE: Pond

LAUNCH INFO:

Bigelow Pond is located within Bigelow Hollow State Park on Route 171 in Union, CT. This pond has an easily accessible boat launch and large parking area that will easily accommodate trailers; it is located on the left side of the main park road near the entrance to the park.

LAST PADDLED: 8/10/14

OUR EXPERIENCES:

We saw several fishermen on Bigelow Hollow Pond, some in kayaks and canoes, others in motorized boats, and one fishing from an inflatable pool chair. We saw one nice bass caught while we were there and another fisherman told us he had been on that pond all day.

I like the picnic areas located along the shoreline of this pond. These areas are both accessible from the water and by using trails and stairs from parking areas along the road leading to Mashapaug Lake. Nice quiet areas to cook up some hot dogs and burgers and relax. Mashapaug lake also has picnicking areas; however, Bigelow Hollow Pond is significantly more private and quiet.

I was disappointed that we didn't see wildlife while paddling on this pond or on the bigger Mashapaug Lake. One ham-bone bullfrog was the extent of the wildlife that we saw while we were on this pond; not really surprising due to the number of people on, and around, this pond! I counted a dozen boats on this small pond, a few people fishing from shore, and a couple of people floating around on blow up rafts.

If venturing to this location, I recommend paddlers make a day of it; have a picnic, and enjoy some of the other activities at this location--like maybe a hike out to Breakneck Pond.

NOTES:

BILLINGS LAKE

STONINGTON, CT

This lake is only 97 acres and primarily a fishing spot; however, it is also a very relaxing and quiet place to paddle and hang-out. Large areas of rock break up the green tree-lined shore and add a bit more interest to this already beautiful spot, and the two bigger islands have fire pits on them. The water is very clear and for the most part weed free; however, there is a small section of lily pads and underwater vegetation towards the far end; but, nothing that hinders paddling.

People can frequently be seen laughing, swimming, and jumping off the rocks directly across from the boat ramp.

TYPE: Pond

LAUNCH INFO:

The boat launch is located at Billings Lake Road (off Rte 201) in North Stonington, CT. It has a wide ramp which allows multiple kayaks to be launched at one time and ample parking for vehicles with trailers.

LAST PADDLED: Summer 2014

OUR EXPERIENCES:

Most recently, eight of us, and my dog, stopped by Buttonwood Farm for homemade ice cream before paddling on Billings Lake. Buttonwood Farm is the go-to ice cream destination in this area and I have been there many times. It is a bit more pricey than others in the area; but, worth it.

Later in the season, the many acres of sunflowers attract tourists to this area as well. The sunflowers can be viewed from the ice cream shop, roadside, and tours are sometimes available. Bunches of sunflowers have been sold during the Sunflower Festival to benefit the Make-A-Wish Foundation. Buttonwood Farm is located at 473 Shetucket Turnpike (Route 165) in Griswold, CT.

Billings Lake. It's primarily a fishing spot, and I can understand why; this is an inviting spot for a lazy afternoon paddle. Having a pole with line in the water makes it all legit--he he he.

One side of the lake belongs to a summer camp so there aren't as many houses as one might expect on this pond. The two bigger islands within this pond each have rustic fire pits and would be peaceful places to have a restful lunch break. We got out on one of the islands and let my dog walk around while we sat and enjoyed the view. We didn't see much wildlife; we saw turtles, fish and a few herons.

There were people swimming off the rocks directly across from the boat ramp when we arrived and different people swimming in the same area when we left. With only 97 acres, paddlers won't get much paddle time or exercise out of this pond; but, sometimes it's not about the exercise. If paddling in the area, Billings Lake might be worth a peek. However, I wouldn't drive any distance to check it out.

BLUFF POINT

GROTON, CT

TYPE: Coastal, island, and beach access

LAUNCH INFO:

Boat Launch is located on Depot Road in the Bluff Point State Park in Groton, CT

LAST PADDLED: 10/20/15.

OUR EXPERIENCES:

I have launched from the Bluff Point launch; however, I have not yet paddled out to the point *(see Bushy Beach on page 49)*. A paddle to the Point is on our paddling schedule for 2016. Join us on Face Book (Kayaking CT with Lou) to receive invitations to paddle with us at this and other locations. *(please, no solicitation)*

NOTES:

Butts Bridge/Quinebaug River in Canterbury, CT
(See page 51)

BOG MEADOW RESERVOIR

EAST KILLINGLY, CT

Paddlers who look out over this pond, are likely to think that it's smaller than it actually is. Paddling straight to the back of Bog Meadow Reservoir and weaving between the sticks and twigs, will bring paddlers to an occupied beaver hut followed by a tunnel that goes under Route 101. Beyond the tunnel, paddlers will find themselves looking out over low falls into Middle Reservoir.

CAUTION: Please stay back from the falls and do not try to cross it; even small falls can be very dangerous, and even life threatening. There is often so much more going on under the water than can be seen on the surface! Flipping at a falls can force the paddler to come in contact with structural issues of the dam that are not readily seen above the surface as well.

Paddling to the back of the pond to where it starts to get sticky (before the beaver hut and tunnel), and then paddling right, leads to a small loop through a marshier grass area where ducks tend to linger.

There are other spots along that side where I've strapped down my paddle and just kept grabbing at the next small twiggy tree, pulling the kayak over the smaller sticks and between the bigger stuff until I reached clearer water again. My dog and I have scared up ducks in these more secluded areas of this pond; not sure what type, but they're not all mallards.

TYPE: Pond/Reservoir

LAUNCH INFO:

There is no formal launch for this pond on Bear Hill Road in East Killingly, CT. We park in a small pull off area on the side of the pond closest to Route 101 and launched from the low grassy embankment. Utilizing this location, requires getting into a floating kayak, although the water is not very deep at the put-in. I've easily launched from this location with my dog on board.

LAST PADDLED: 10/28/14

OUR EXPERIENCES:

As a teenager, I spent countless hours on this pond fishing and hanging out with my friends. I last paddled this pond with my dog during the 2015 paddling season to see if the beavers were still active in the area.

This is the smallest of the 5 East Killingly Reservoirs and probably not worth paddling unless fishing or feeling nostalgic. However, it might be worth a peek when paddling in the area. There are also a few other smaller ponds on the same road, and within view of this pond, that are too small for paddling: but, may still be good for fishing from shore. The other five Killingly reservoirs are only minutes away: *See separate entries for Eddy Pray, Killingly Pond, Alvia Chase Reservoir, and Middle Reservoir.*

NOTES:

BROCKWAY ISLAND
CONNECTICUT RIVER

ESSEX/LYME, CT

Brockway Island is a very small narrow island located at the mouth of Hamburg Cove on the Connecticut River. This island is a landmark for the opening of Hamburg Cove and it has a massive expanse of exposed beach at low tide. The beach area is on the Connecticut River side of the island and the sand is fine and goes on and on.

Note: there is a house *(rental)* located on the opposite side of the island. I don't know if the island is open to the public or privately owned. We stayed on the (low tide) beach facing the Connecticut River and we did not see any signs indicating that this was not allowed.

TYPE: Island, Tidal River

LAUNCH INFO:

We paddled down river to Brockway Island and beyond after camping out on Selden Island; however, paddlers can access this area from some of the local marinas. The area surrounding this island could also be accessed from nearby Hamburg Cove *(See page 91).* I have also paddled upriver from this area to Castle Marina *(river right of Selden Island)* with the incoming tide.

LAST PADDLED: 8/27/15

OUR EXPERIENCES:

There were people swimming with their dogs when we arrived at low tide, and I walked Brockway's beach among a large flock of seagulls; some of which, were laying down and didn't even bother to get up. Very relaxing place with a great view of large and small sailboats, as well as other boats, going up and down river.

If paddling in the area of Brockway Island, I suggest entering at least the beginning of Hamburg Cove *(See page 91)*. In the initial opening of the cove (before the boats) we saw deer, heron, geese, an eagle, cormorants and egrets! Badabing! We saw many birds in Hamburg Cove including an up close and personal with an eagle. We found that the main concentration of birds was in the mouth of Hamburg Cove and near Brockway Island.

NOTES:

BUSHY BEACH

GROTON, CT

Bushy Beach is a narrow one mile stretch of beach that faces the Groton Airport, the mouth of the Poquonnock River, and the Sound on the opposite side. This long narrow beach which stretches across the opening of the Poquonnock River, significantly narrows the river's direct contact with the Sound.

The beach's visual vantage point allows paddlers to view planes entering and leaving the airport, the area coast line, two islands, Bluff Point, and the Sound. This is a great place to survey these waterways and plan future paddling adventures while enjoying a picnic lunch.

Note: *We were there at low tide. I have read that the peninsula known as Bushy Beach is an island at high tide.*

TYPE: Coastal Beach

LAUNCH INFO:

Boat Launch is located on Depot Road in the Bluff Point State Park in Groton, CT

LAST PADDLED: 10/20/15

OUR EXPERIENCES:

Three of us paddled from the Bluff Point Boat Launch to Bushy Beach in Groton, CT. It was our intent to do some plane spotting and to paddle out to Bluff Point; however, the wind had picked up and was continuing to increase as we paddled, so we stopped at Bushy Beach.

I would suggest a walk, or perhaps lunch, on Bushy Beach even if planning to paddle to the islands or Bluff Point. It definitely has a great vantage point for plane spotting with the Groton Airport right there!

Even if paddlers are not intending to leave the protected cove area at the mouth of the Poquonnock River, I suggest using a full skirt and a sea kayak. I was getting wave water inside my kayak as I was putting on my skirt at the launch. The onset of wind can significantly increase waves in this area! As is the case with all tidal areas, wind and tide can quickly change paddling conditions, so it's best to be prepared.

I would not suggest leaving the more protected mouth of the Poquonnock River unless paddlers are seasoned coastal and open water paddlers who are properly equipped, and very familiar with the paddling conditions found in the Sound.

NOTES:

BUTTS BRIDGE: QUINEBAUG RIVER

CANTERBURY, CT

Butts Bridge can be used as a put-in to venture up or down river or as a take-out when paddling from northern locations, such as Canterbury Bridge/Robert Manship Park *(Page 175)*, the Killingly Launch *(Page 162)*, and the Plainfield Launch near the fish hatchery *(Page 164)*.

Paddling up river from Butts Bridge after the spring thaw is typically impossible unless there has been very little precipitation over the winter months. Later in the summer months, this section of the river is often smooth like glass. This river becomes more shallow, and the current typically subsides, as the season progresses; however, this section of the river is usually passable through out the season with a kayak.

Directly north of Butts Bridge, is the launch at Canterbury Bridge/ Robert Manship Park Launch *(Page 175)*. The paddle from Canterbury Bridge to Butts Bridge is about 2 1/2 hour paddle with the usually light spring current; more if paddling with me because I like to investigate and watch for birds and wildlife. Even with the typical spring current, paddling is usually necessary. Later in the season there will be more paddling involved and the trip may take longer; of course, unusually high precipitation can change this.

Aspinook Pond is the take-out south of Butts Bridge; however, paddling from Butts Bridge to Aspinook is so quick that I would not recommend spending the time setting up that paddle. I would only use Aspinook if coming down from a more northern launch. *(See Aspinook Pond page 21)*

Even rivers that are typically slow and meandering, can quickly change when other variables like wind and other weather conditions are added..

TYPE: River, Bird/Wildlife Watching

LAUNCH INFO:

The Butts Bridge launch is located at the end of a bumpy dirt road next to the large green metal bridge on Butts Bridge Road in Canterbury, CT. Ample parking and plenty of room for boat trailers.

LAST PADDLED: 3/20/16

OUR EXPERIENCES:

This is one of my favorite fresh water paddling destinations. I try to make the paddle from Canterbury Bridge or the Plainfield Launch down to Butts Bridge, sometimes passing Butts Bridge to Aspinook Pond, every spring. It's a relaxing paddle that unfolds, presenting beauty and wildlife, if paddlers are quiet and observant. I've watched feeding eagles and osprey, muskrats busily swimming about, deer, and most recently, signs of beaver in the area. Our dog, Tiny, eagerly stands on deck watching for the next bird or critter to show itself.

Later in the season, when the current has softened, I paddle up river from Butts Bridge. This is a perfect place for a mental health day or fishing! I've paddled up river and floated in these secluded surroundings with only my dog, my lunch, camera, and a book. I have also done kayak metal detecting on this river and I sometimes encounter fishermen and other recreational paddlers.

I have seen large speed boats and jet skis occasionally enter the waters surrounding Butts Bridge; however, this is rare and they don't typically venture too far north of Butts Bridge. Upriver from this location becomes much shallower with more unpredictable obstacles under the water that are more easily avoided by paddlers.

CHASE RESERVOIR

KILLINGLY, CT

Chase Reservoir is primarily a bass fishing spot and I've seen keep-able bass taken from this pond. For the most part, the shoreline is lined with trees and is pretty much the same all the way around it. There are a few homes located along one side/corner of the reservoir, but they are set back from the water and are not usually visible during the paddling season unless paddling very close to them.

TYPE: Reservoir/Pond, Bass Fishing

LAUNCH INFO:

The boat Launch is located on Pratt Road (off Rte 101) in East Killingly, CT. We park on the dirt road (left entry) and carry our kayaks down one of the paths to the water.

LAST PADDLED: 5/18/14

OUR EXPERIENCES:

There were 12 kayaks, 1 rowboat, and 2 canoes on the water during our most recent trip to this location; however, a weekday might be less active than a Sunday afternoon. There were too many people fishing from shore and in boats that day to really see much wildlife. We explored the reservoir for a few hours and saw everything. We found 2 stone walls beneath the water and an occasional heron and turtle. We did see keep-able bass caught that day.

Evidently, swans can dance!
(Quinebaug River; see page 159)

COVENTRY LAKE

COVENTRY, CT

Coventry Lake is around 370 acres and it is very heavily populated; in some areas there are houses behind houses and then houses behind those houses! I couldn't get over the number of houses lining the shores of this lake! This lake is really a sit-n-spin with only a couple of inlet areas that can't be seen from the center of the lake. This lake might be good for fishing or perhaps some paddling exercise.

TYPE: Lake

LAUNCH INFO:

The Coventry Lake boat launch is located on 30 Cross Street in Coventry, CT. It has a cement ramp, a dock, and a nice parking area.

LAST PADDLED: 10/13/14

OUR EXPERIENCES:

Despite the fact that it is so heavily populated and it is a sit-n-spin lake, we did paddle around this lake. We did see a few gulls, geese, and baby cormorants. I have been told that there is good fishing at Coventry Lake. I recommend recreational kayakers, and those interested in birding/wildlife, check out nearby Eagleville Lake *(Page 59)*. Eagleville Lake is only a couple of minutes away and also has river access!

TIP FOR BEGINNERS

Paddlers who do not know how to execute the two paddling maneuvers used to stop a kayak from flipping, should ask a kayaking instructor or other knowledgeable and experienced paddler to show them how to do these maneuvers. There are some informative videos on You Tube: however, in-person instruction would be better. There are two very easily learned paddling maneuvers that can stop a kayak from tipping over in many situations; but, they only work if the paddler knows how to do them!

DOANEVILLE POND

GRISWOLD, CT

The only public access to this 68 acre pond is through Glasgo Pond in Glasgo, CT. There is a mobile home park on the left as paddlers pass under the bridge and enter the pond; however, the remainder of the pond is sparsely populated. There is a flock of geese on this pond that will typically allow paddlers to float very close to them and observe them if paddlers are quiet and patient.

TYPE: Pond

LAUNCH INFO:

The only public access to this 68 acre pond is through Glasgo Pond. The Glasgo Pond launch is located at 45 Hillview Heights in Griswold, CT. Paddle left from the Glasgo Pond public boat ramp, continuing to bear left as paddlers enter the main body of water. Continue to follow the right bend in the water way until paddlers reach the Sheldon Road bridge; after crossing under the bridge, paddlers will be in Doaneville Pond.

LAST PADDLED: 7/22/14

OUR EXPERIENCES:

We enjoyed the Canada Geese very much. They hesitantly exited up the embankment from the shore when we arrived in their area; but, then they ran back down the embankment and flew into the water around us after observing us for only a few moments! Spectacular! These geese will come reasonably close to paddlers who are quiet, respectful, and patient. They even approached my kayak with my dog onboard! Allow them to come to you, please! I did not feed them; however, I believe they are accustomed to being fed by humans.

We also saw hawks, turtles, frogs and even a fish jumping with its entire body breaching the surface during our late afternoon visit. My dog really enjoyed the geese during this paddle. Please respect the wildlife; bring binoculars so that you are not tempted to intrude upon their personal space!

NOTES:

EAGLEVILLE LAKE

COVENTRY, CT

At first glance, this almost 80 acre pond appears to be less than what actually awaits paddlers who stop to visit. This location provides access to the Willimantic River and can be used as a take-out from more northern put-ins such as Heron Cove *(See Heron Cove entry page 95),* or paddlers can paddle the lake and then paddle up river a bit from this location.

Finding the river access while paddling this pond can be a bit tricky because there is a maze of grasses, islands, and such towards the back of the pond--keep searching, you'll find it. The shoreline of this lake turns a magnificent deep red color when the leaves change in the fall.

TYPE: Lake, Bass Fishing, River Access, Fall Foliage

LAUNCH INFO:

The steep stone and cement launch is located to the left of the dam/falls at 30 Pine Lake Drive in Coventry, CT. This launch is probably good for launching motor boats, however, it leaves a lot to be desired when launching kayaks. On one occasion when we used this launch as a take-out for a Willimantic River paddle, one of our paddlers fell in at this launch! This wasn't a big surprise to me because I never actually use this launch; it's steep with random rocks poking up from the bottom where the ramp meets the water. I launch and exit slightly to the left of it when facing the water.

LAST PADDLED: April 2015

OUR EXPERIENCES:

During our latest paddle around Eagleville Lake, we encountered 5 fishermen out on the pond; 2 said they caught a single nice bass each. The person who was fishing in our group got a couple of bites, but no solid hits. Along the way, we found a beaver lodge with recent cuttings showing proof of their existence on this pond. We also saw ducks, cormorants, herons, and turtles. This pond is very shallow and weedy in some areas.

I recommend a fall paddle at this location because the red foliage is spectacular!

See Heron Cove entry for information regarding down river paddling to this site (Page 95).

NOTES:

EDDY PRAY RESERVOIR

EAST KILLINGLY, CT

Eddy Pray Reservoir is a hidden treasure of North Eastern Connecticut and is one of five reservoirs clustered together in East Killingly CT. The five reservoirs are Eddy Pray Reservoir, Old Killingly Pond (Killingly Pond), Middle Reservoir, Alvia Chase Reservoir and lastly the one we referred to as "The Bog" growing up. "The Bog's" formal name is Bog Meadow Reservoir. Of the five ponds, Eddy Pray Reservoir is by far my favorite.

This secluded reservoir is difficult to find; but, well worth the effort for those paddlers who love to explore or fish and have a couple of hours to do so. *See our experiences on page 63.*

To the back/left of the reservoir, paddlers will find a good example of water being over taken by patches of mud, some with grass and plants starting to grow on them. The smaller patches can be slid over or pushed apart with a paddle while the larger ones just need to be avoided. We saw two heron, a king fisher, swallows, red wing black birds, and some other birds back there. Binoculars are a must!

The launch at this site is probably as rustic a launch as many will ever encounter in this area and it may not be advisable for paddlers with certain health conditions. *Please read launch info on the following page for details.* Use this launch and paddle at your own risk and discretion. Only you can determine what is and is not safe and appropriate for your level of experience and condition.

TYPE: Reservoir, Bird/Wildlife Watching, Fishing

LAUNCH INFO:

Informal rustic launch: Take North Road from Rte 101 in East Killingly, then turn right onto Quinns Hill Road. Eddy Pray Reservoir will be out of sight on the left side of the dirt/gravel road. Carefully watch for two large rocks and an opening with pallets laid out on the ground just to the right of a telephone pole.

Eddy Pray Reservoir, East Killingly, CT

The uphill path and launch area are as rustic as rustic can be; however, the trek across the pallets, and up and then down the hill, are well worth the feeling of peacefulness and "being away from it all" that comes from kayaking on this reservoir *(See our experiences below)*. I suggest that people with physically limiting health conditions or disabilities carefully consider other options or bring someone who can carry their kayak up and down the hill, to and from the water, and assist them with getting onto/out of the water.

LAST PADDLED: 7/13/14

OUR EXPERIENCES:

Paddlers truly get the illusion of being away from it all here. No traffic or modern day noise. There are moments when no fish jump and no birds chirp and true silence can be experienced. The only indicator of civilization is the appearance of the North Road tower in the distance, a large white drainage pipe...and the kayaks.

On our most recent visit, we met 2 fishermen who were leaving as we were arriving, but saw no other people during the 2 hours that we were there. We visited on a weekday afternoon.

I first visited Eddy Pray Reservoir as a teenager and I'm pleased to say that it still has that same old time feel to it....like escaping to simpler times. Great relaxing place to paddle for a few hours on a nice summer day! --if you can find it!

RIVER PADDLING TIP

A paddle leash is an inexpensive item which makes retrieving a dropped paddle a lot easier than chasing it down river. It is basically a para Cord or piece of rope that is attached to both the paddle and the kayak. A paddle leash can be purchased or made; however, paddlers who choose to make one, should be sure that it is long enough to effectively use the paddle; but, not so long that it could become twisted around the paddler's neck or other body part should the kayak flip. I suggest paddlers purchase one from a reputable kayak supply source or check the dimensions and length of kayak paddle leashes sold by reputable kayak equipment suppliers before making one.

I've made several from narrow rope with a sewn closed loop to go over the paddle handle at one end and a clip at the other end; however, I currently have one that I quickly made from Para Cord because I keep giving the good ones away to people who don't yet have one.

FITCHVILLE POND
YANTIC RIVER ACCESS

BOZRAH, CT

Fitchville Pond has something to offer in regard to birding and fishing if paddlers can get past the constant traffic noise! In some areas the traffic noise is very loud, while in other areas it is more like a constant droning background noise; however, it was always present at some level. I found it to be a distraction that didn't allow me to fully relax.

TYPE: Pond with limited Yantic River access, Camping

LAUNCH INFO:

This informal launch is adjacent to a dirt pull off area near, but not next to, the bridge on Bozrah Street Ext in Bozrah, CT. This road crosses in between the two halves of this pond. The launch is very steep; my kayak almost launched itself going down that hill and I was grateful to the young boy who helped me carry my kayak back up that hill. Paddlers camping at the campground across the pond can launch from there

Paddlers using this launch can look across the pond and see Odetah Campground which is located at 38 Bozrah Street Extension in Bozrah, CT. http://www.odetah.com/

LAST PADDLED: 8/5/15

OUR EXPERIENCES:

After spending a significant amount of time watching an egret preen itself about 30 feet in front of my kayak, I saw an animal's rounded back floating in the distance. I thought the animal that belonged to the fur showing above the surface was likely dead; however, as I paddled closer, I saw it was very busily doing something under water with its rounded back showing above the weedy surface. I coasted right up along side and poked it to be sure it wasn't trapped and in need of assistance. LOL!

The muskrat startled, stretched out, shot me a look without ever breaking the water's surface, and swam under my kayak and away. I will never forget that face, and I chuckle every time I think of this experience. Not sure what he was doing in the weeds; but, whatever it was, it had 100% of its attention! I did see trail like paths, equal to about its width, making their way through the thick weeds in that area; so, perhaps he was eating his way through the weeds?

Paddlers will have to look for the birds! I didn't see the majority of them until I had paddled most of the pond and part of the river. I saw the geese near the campground and an egret and heron up past the campground in a little more secluded lily pad covered area. I saw one muskrat and a flock of ducks up river. There is an area that birding paddlers should not over look when entering the second section of the pond; the dam will be to the right--go left, then instead of going up river, stay to the left and go into that long inlet area. That is where I saw an egret, heron, many birds, and I touched the muskrat!

This is a place of bridges. I paddled the pond and up river to the Colchester Turnpike Bridge (walked the last 1/2 mile pulling my kayak because the water was too low) and I went under a total of 5 bridges! The two very high bridges that cross the pond gave me a few moments of awe looking up at them as I paddled the narrow passage from one section of the pond to the other.

FIVE MILE RIVER:

DAYVILLE TO DANIELSON, CT

The Five Mile River is often over looked because only portions of it can be successfully paddled, and the most optimal time is after the spring thaw. This is a very relaxing paddle down a narrow winding river with only a few areas where the current momentarily picks up some speed. There are a variety of birds in the area and even otter can be seen near the old stone bridge! During a 2014 paddle at this location, one paddler caught a 2 lb brown trout at the launch before we even started! Yes, a brown trout!

This section of the Five Mile River could also be a good paddle for an experienced flat water paddler who is looking for some intro level river paddling. Rivers can be trickier than they appear to be when paddlers don't know what to expect; so, I suggest novice paddlers bring an experienced river paddler with them when paddling at this location.

TYPE: River, Bird/Wildlife Watching, Trout & Bass Fishing

LAUNCH INFO:

Put in: This informal launch is located at the bridge on the Route 12 end of Rock Ave in Dayville, CT. Paddlers can park in the large open dirt area, cross the street, and launch in the area adjacent to the bridge. There is a steep short slope to the water before it levels out. In the spring, paddlers might need to cut back the pickers at the launch if they are the first to arrive; later in the season, this will usually have been done by other paddlers.

Take out for this trip is the public launch located at the foot bridge on Water Street in Danielson, CT. Paddling down river from Rock Ave, the launch will be river left after passing under the foot bridge. This launch is easier to maneuver than the steep put-in and there is ample parking spaces at this locations. Paddling to and from the lower launch is usually possible later in the season. Keep in mind storms, wind, and high or low water levels could change this.

LAST PADDLED: 3/22/16

OUR EXPERIENCES:

Our last 2016 paddle took about 3 hours, pausing occasionally to fish and watch wildlife; so, this section probably could be paddled straight through in about 2 1/2 hours. We maneuvered over logs and sticks beneath the water that would become even more exposed to the surface as water levels continue to recede throughout the summer. Downed trees had been cut back to provide continued paddling.

During a 2015 paddle, the 2 lb brown trout and the bass that got away were neat, however, seeing the otter was the highlight of that trip. We passed under the stone bridge; but, I went back because the sun shadowed that side of the bridge and the photos I took were too dark. As I passed back under the bridge, the otter and I were face to face! It probably thought we had left and it was safe to come out. We both had an auuuh moment before it grumbled a few otter words and slipped into the water.

We also saw a tiny baby swan, a very territorial swan (known to be aggressive) that attempted to chase us for a bit near the entrance of Five Mile Pond, a nesting swan on the tiny island in that same area, ducks, turtles...and a bass that flipped up, and as it broke the surface of the water, ditched the hook, and got away. That's the bass fish story...and I'm stickin' to it!

FIVE MILE RIVER:

PUTNAM TO PINEVILLE, CT

As I said in the previous entry, the Five Mile River is often over looked because only portions of it can be successfully paddled and the most optimal time is after the spring thaw. This is an amazing section of river for paddlers who are into wildlife and who can paddle in stealth mode! I once had a buck deer leap into the water behind my kayak and cross the river as I attempted to sneak up on a beaver while paddling through a narrow pass-through. My dog and I were close enough to get wet from the resulting splash!

This paddle should be done early in the season after the spring thaw. However, I sometimes use this section of this river as our annual over the beaver dam river challenge later in the season. At that time, paddlers must portage downed trees and several small to very large beaver dams. I thought I counted seven dams; however, last summer, one paddler assured me that there were 10!

In the early spring, this paddle is moderately challenging; later in the season, paddlers will know that they had a serious work out if they try to paddle this section of river! I would recommend bringing a GPS or using a GPS APP on a phone because there is at least one area where paddlers will be guessing which way to go if they are not already familiar with this section of river. Both ways look very inviting; paddlers will cross quite a distance, and at least a few obstacles, before realizing whether they picked the right course. If for some reason you do not have your GPS or your phone gets wet--over the dam, not the downed tree!

TYPE: Rustic river conditions, abundant wildlife

LAUNCH INFO:

The put-in launch is located at the small park on Route 44 in Putnam, CT where the Five Mile River crosses under it (on the right just past Munyan Road when arriving from downtown Putnam/Rte 395); there is plenty of parking, a couple of picnic tables, a rope swing (famous to all locals), and entry to the Five Mile River.

At this location, there is a path to the right of the parking area that can be used by paddlers to check the conditions of the river and water level at different points before entering the river. This section of river is usually most shallow in the area at the start of that path; so, if it looks too low there, it may only get slightly easier below that point.

It has been many years since I've launched above the park in Putnam. The further up river that one launches, the more difficult the paddle. The next put-in is at the Munyan Road Bridge. Paddlers should be certain that they are viewing the Five Mile River and not Munson Brook because both cross Munyan Road and the brook will be too shallow. There is no formal launch or parking, and launching will require more work than launching at the park in Putnam.

Putting in above Munyan Road is limited to very early spring and involves rock dodging, possibly some portaging, and a small section of rapids. It's also possible for paddlers to put in, be on their way, only to find they're bottoming out and not able to easily proceed forward or back without getting out and pulling or carrying kayaks. This section is difficult and should not be attempted by beginners and those who are not very familiar with paddling these types of conditions.

Paddle at your own risk and discretion; only you can determine what is, or is not, safe and appropriate for you and your level of experience and condition. It is your responsibility to determine the legality, suitability, and safety of paddling at the destinations and paddling routes in this book.

Take-out in Pineville on River Road.

This launch from the road: This launch is located on River Road between the North Road Bridge and Putnam Road in Pineville, CT. The path to the launch is located between two large boulders adjacent to the long dirt pull off area on the river side of the road.

I suggest that paddlers walk down the path and look across the river because there is a section of wall/foundation that is a good landmark for recognizing the launch when paddling down river. This take-out is initially steep, then levels out to a rocky water's edge. Getting in/out of a kayak at this location is easiest if paddlers step into the water to do so rather than trying to stay dry and step in/out to the shore.

There are a couple of fishing areas between this launch and the River Road bridge that would require less walking to launch; however, the parking pull off area doesn't extend that far.

From the river: This launch is river right a short distance after passing under the North Road Bridge. Paddlers can paddle past this take out point and go under the River Road bridge and then back track to this take out point when water level and current permit; but, be aware that there is a dam/falls only a short distance after the bridge and it is an unmarked spill way. There are no buoys or warnings to show that it is there other than the sound of the water going over it. The water pools into a pond like area after the bridge before the dam/falls which may be good for fishing? STAY BACK FROM THE FALLS!

Paddle at your own risk and discretion; only you can determine what is, or is not, safe and appropriate for you and your level of experience and condition. It is your responsibility to determine the legality, suitability, and safety of paddling at the destinations and paddling routes in this book

LAST PADDLED: 7/21/15

OUR EXPERIENCES:

Our July over the beaver dam challenge paddle took 4 hours; however, we launched in Putnam and then paddled upriver before paddling back down river to Pineville. If paddled after a spring thaw, the resulting current would likely be stronger, and may hinder or prevent paddling upriver and a down river paddle would take less time.

The Chase Road Bridge was still under construction *(summer 2015)*. Paddling through the open channel under the bridge during non-work hours was uneventful; however, during work hours, paddlers should signal workers and let them know they're there, and would like to pass, before approaching the bridge. Might be helpful to have a whistle to get their attention if machinery is being operated. Passing while machinery is being operated can be extremely dangerous, even life threatening; so, if they're working, please don't pass without first notifying them of your desire to do so!

Our paddler on point saw deer. We also saw the usual heron and ducks as well. Paddlers who are looking to see wildlife, should paddle with one or two people who can be very quiet! I sometimes make this paddle with only my dog because I see significantly more wildlife than if I have other paddlers with me.

During a recent paddle on the lower section of this route, I paddled upriver from the lower launch on River Road and saw deer, beaver, heron, and turkeys. This was the trip where the deer leaped into the water behind my kayak while I was sneaking up on a beaver. I slowly pulled my way through the cut-off, expecting to see the beaver that frequents that area; but, instead I saw a doe and fawn in the distance drinking from the river. I blurted out a sigh and the buck rose from the thicket directly behind me and leaped into the water, crossing the river. Of course the doe and fawn ran...and a heron flew. I could live to be old and senile; but, I'll never forget that experience and it will always bring a smile to my face!

GARDNER LAKE

SALEM, CT

Gardner Lake borders the towns of Bozrah, Salem, and Montville, CT. This lake is a little over 5 acres and known for its bass and walleye fishing. It also has two unique points of interest.

Minnie island can be seen to the right just after leaving the launch area. This island consists of less than one acre of wooded land which slopes up hill to its center. It is notably the smallest State Park in Connecticut. The island has a 2 very rustic points of entry and is, for the most part, heavily wooded.

If that is not interesting enough, the sunken house will certainly pique your curiosity. In the late 1800s, a man decided to move his house over the ice from one shore of the lake to another. Different sources report a slightly different series of events; however, all stories end with the house going through the ice and settling on the lake bottom with the owner's piano, furniture, and other belongings still inside.

Several sources report that local children would play in its attic and jump into the water from its roof during the summer months; these same children enjoyed skating about the exposed part of the house in winter. The house eventually sank below the surface and has deteriorated over time. Scuba divers have reportedly removed objects from this site.

TYPE: Lake, Bass and Walleye Fishing

LAUNCH INFO:

This DEEP launch is located on Route 354/Old Colchester Turnpike near Route 82 in Salem, CT. The launch is identified with a state sign. It is a really nice launch with ample parking, seasonal chemical toilets, an attached beach area, and picnic tables.

LAST PADDLED: 4/17/16

OUR EXPERIENCES:

We enjoyed paddling around Gardner Lake; however, motor boats were a constant on this lake throughout the day. Whenever, one or two left, a few more would show up to take their place. We paddled on a week day afternoon in late April and saw many empty docks in addition to the boats that were in use on the water; so, it is very likely that this lake is busy during the summer months.

Its shoreline is moderately populated on the launch side of the lake and less so towards the back of the lake. The houses and trailer parks on this lake are well maintained and easy on the eyes.

As we paddled past Minnie Island we saw three kayaks on its shore. The owners of those kayaks were busily setting up a tent at the top center of the island. The top of this island offers paddlers a great view of that part of the lake.

The lake water was like glass when we set out in the morning; but, became quite choppy later when the wind picked up and the number of motor boats increased. I suggest a skirt or paddling pants on colder windy days where paddlers might be uncomfortable after getting wet. We paddled around the lake, stopping in one of the back inlet areas for coffee and snack. We were on the water for about 5 hours.

GLASGO POND

GRISWOLD, CT

Glasgo Pond is 168 acres and might be of little interest for anything other than fishing or swimming if it were merely a typical round or oval pond; but, its long and irregular shaped and its connection to Doaneville Pond makes it more interesting to explore.

Paddling right from the boat launch, paddlers will enter a short length of water which includes a small cliff area where children often jump into, and swim in, the water below it; to the left of this cliff is the falls (*stay back*). About half-way between the rope swing *(located directly across from the launch)* and the rock cliff area to the right, is an old cemetery up on the hill. Sometimes, a few headstones and flags placed near them can be seen if trees and other foliage are not blocking the view

Leaving the boat ramp and paddling to the left will bring paddlers into the main body of water. After entering this area, paddlers will see a bridge slightly to the right in the distance. I duck down and walk my hands along the under side of the Route 165 bridge to get to the other side and I'm usually rewarded with being able to follow and watch a family of swans. *Caution swans can become aggressive, especially when nesting or swimming with young.*

The area beyond the bridge looks shallow; however, poking a paddle down into it will demonstrate that some areas are actually deep. This illusion is created because the vegetation is thick and grows close to the water's surface. About 1/2 of this area beyond the bridge is most often covered in lily pads and other weeds.

The swans are very accommodating and have allowed me to view them foraging for food and interacting as a family. Please respect the wildlife. It would be a shame to spoil this experience for others! *Swans can be very territorial, and sometimes aggressive, especially when young are involved.*

After returning to the main body of water and paddling to the right, paddlers will pass the most populated area of the pond and eventually arrive at a bridge. Passing under the bridge will take paddlers into Doaneville Pond *(Page 57)*. This under bridge access is the only public entrance to the smaller Doaneville Pond. I have enjoyed close and extended interactions with a flock of Canada geese on this pond.

NOTE: Sometimes Glasgo Pond is drained so that work can be done to the dam.

TYPE: Pond

LAUNCH INFO:

The launch is located at 45 Hillview Heights in Griswold, CT. It has a large parking area and a nice hard surface launch; however, the dirt road leading up to it is usually full of pot holes, so drive slow.

LAST PADDLED: July 2015

OUR EXPERIENCES:

Glasgo Pond brings out, and fosters, the child within me. When I arrived at the pond during my last paddle, I was greeted by teenagers swimming at the boat launch where it very clearly says, "NO

Swimming." A young boy on the rope swing proudly announced his 11th birthday and that he was going to try the swing for the first time! They were all deeply involved in a charming world of childhood fun and even disregarded an adult bystander's warning against making the jump; undaunted, the child swung and let go of the rope!

The jumper and all onlookers were rewarded with yells of victory and pride as the 11 year old delivered a perfect splash! Their triumphant cheers were then matched by whistles and shouts of encouragement from the children jumping from the rock cliff further down to the right! One can't help but remember what it was like to be eleven years old and leave the launch area smiling.

As I returned to the boat launch, I was once again warmly greeted by a young child fishing with his family. Upon my arrival, he announced that the fish hook being removed from his finger was "OK" because he had a tetanus shot and then continued to tell me why fish like meal worms. This is often a charming and nostalgic place for a family paddle.

NOTES:

SAFETY TIP

It's a good idea for paddlers to let someone know where they're going to be paddling, who will be going, and when they plan to be back. Paddlers can then text this person when they arrive at their launch destination, if plans change, and when they're on their way back. This can be a very quick text, saying, "On the water, out of the water, on my way to..., and home." The paddler could also give this contact person the number of at least one other person in their group so that the contact person has an alternate way to get in touch if the paddler cannot be reached. I do this every time I paddle.

If a paddler is several hours late getting home and nobody knows where to look for them, they're not answering their phone, and nobody knows who went on the paddle or where they've been, it's going to be a lot harder to find and help that paddler! In a life threatening emergency, this information could be the difference between life and death.

GREAT ISLAND WILDLIFE PRESERVE:

CONNECTICUT RIVER

OLD LYME, CT

The Great Island Preserve is located near the mouth of the Connecticut River and is only accessible by boat. The island is separated from the launch by a narrow canal like water way with the Connecticut River on the opposite side. This area, including the back passage paddle from Great Island to the Lieutenant River *(See featured entry page 7),* is a fabulous birding location. In season, paddlers can even watch adult osprey feeding young on the many nesting platforms.

TYPE: Island Wildlife Preserve, Tidal River, Bird Watching

CAUTION:

Tidal Area: All tidal area precautions apply. This site is located near the mouth of the Connecticut River and Long Island Sound.

View from a beach on the Connecticut River side of Great Island.

LAUNCH INFO:

The launch area is located at 99 Smith Neck Road (off Rte 156) in Old Lyme, CT and is 500' from Great Island. Nice parking area, turning area, and ramp. In addition to close and almost immediate access to Great Island Wildlife Preserve, this launch also provides an access point for the mouth of the Connecticut River, Long Island Sound, and places like the Black Hall River. It can also be used as a take-out for a down river paddle.

LAST PADDLED: Summer 2015 (3x)

OUR EXPERIENCES:

During our 3 hour paddle around the island we saw several osprey and some of them feeding young! We saw swans with babies (that could fit in the palm of my hand) swimming in the channel between the island and the mainland, along with several other birds, like egrets, snowy egrets, red wing black birds, cormorants, sand pipers, and a large flock of sea gulls.

We paddled around the entire island and strolled a couple of the beach areas on the far side of the island (*photo facing page).* The birds on that side of the island seemed to be limited to gulls and sand pipers. We saw the majority of the birds in the waterway between the island and the mainland and in little inlet areas off that waterway. This is a beautiful area with lots of birds for those paddlers who are into kayak birding!

The waterway between the island and the mainland was smooth paddling; however, the CT River side of the island had waves which were easily paddled by experienced kayakers. No motorized boats came near the island while we were there; however, there were two occasions when two very large boats passed through at the same time on the opposite side of the river, creating a couple of waves that splashed over the top of my kayak, sloshing up to and over my shoulder, soaking me! Getting wet in 91 degree weather was a treat; however, I could picture this situation causing some amount of concern for less experienced paddlers. Due to the increased height of the waves when large boats pass through, I recommend a kayak skirt when paddling the open river side of the island.

Paddlers who think this might not be a laughable moment, should stay in the area between the island and the mainland or wear a PFD, put a skirt on their kayak, and bring an experienced tidal river paddler with them. Do not attempt to paddle this area with a kayak that is inappropriate for the situation. An ocean kayak would be best suited for paddling the outer side of the island. If paddling towards Long Island Sound, paddlers should definitely have an ocean kayak and skirt.

BUGS: There were biting gnat-like flying insects. A light spray on our arms and the problem was solved. I've been told that this situation gets more intense as the season progresses, so bring bug spray.

NOTES:

GREEN FALLS:
PACHAUG FOREST

VOLUNTOWN, CT

Green Falls has an enchanting quality about it that allows the kayaker to let go of the every day hustle and bustle of the world and stay in the present, enjoying each moment as it arrives. The absence of houses and other structures gives the kayaker a sense of being far from civilization while at the same time not having to drive far to get there. This location has an easily accessible boat ramp, parking, camping, fishing, and hiking.

The shoreline is a blend of rock, trees, and vegetation. Two islands and one rock formation jutting from the surface offer an interesting element that some other nearby lakes and reservoirs don't. There are several places that allow paddlers the option of exiting the water to explore along the shoreline, view the small falls, and enter the small islands.

TYPE: State Forest, Camping, Swimming, Fishing, Boating

LAUNCH INFO:

Very accessible boat launch in the Pachaug State Forest off Route 138 (Green Falls Pond Road) in Voluntown, CT. Watch for Pachaug State Forest sign on Route 138. **Note**: After exiting the main road, it is more than a 2 mile ride to the boat launch so don't be too quick to think you went the wrong way. I recommend using GPS. Closed to boaters at sunset.

CAMPING:

Campsites are first come--first get and available from the last week in April to end of September. A park employee will be around to collect camping fees. It can be difficult, if not impossible to get a site on weekends during the peak camping season. Nearby MT Misery Campground, on Route 49, is sometimes a good secondary option when Green Falls campground is full; however, it does not have the immediate water access available at Green Falls. I've enjoyed camping at this location many times. It is a DEEP site.

LAST PADDLED: 6/19/14

OUR EXPERIENCES:

During our last visit to this location, we paddled Green Falls on a weekday afternoon. Three of us arrived on the water at about 2:30 pm and explored until sunset at 8:30 pm. We ventured out onto some of the islands and walked part of the trail that goes around the pond.

We were told no fish had been caught YET and one fisherman admitted to enjoying being out in the sunshine more than the need to catch fish. There were a few other people out on the pond with both boats and kayaks, and laughter and giggling could be heard emanating from the swimming area while we paddled the pond.

I have camped at this location many times; however, it can be difficult to secure a spot because it is a popular summer retreat due to the variety of activities available at this location.

NOTES:

GREENVILLE DAM: SHETUCKET RIVER

NORWICH, CT

Caution this is a functioning hydro-electric dam/plant that sometimes holds back and releases significant amounts of water; a horn will blast to warn paddlers to get themselves and their equipment out of the water until the water levels out again. Paddlers who do not have significant river paddling experience and extensive knowledge of this river should not paddle on the Shetucket River unless accompanied by an experienced river guide who possess extensive knowledge and experience paddling this river. Paddlers should always wear an emergency whistle and PFD when paddling any part of the Shetucket River.

The Greenville Dam is a portage area for down river paddling on the Shetucket and Thames Rivers. Next take-out after the Greenville Dam is on the Thames River at the Howard Brown Memorial Park in Norwich *(See page 101)* . Paddlers have additional take-out options along the Thames River *(See page 203)*

It is possible during some times of the year, and within some conditions, to paddle up river to the back side of the Ponemah Mill in Taftville, then returning to the Greenville Dam launch/portage area *(See our experiences below)*. Paddlers won't often escape the sound of traffic when paddling this section of river; however, the area above the Greenville Dam is rich in history and a great wildlife and birding experience.

TYPE: River, Birding, Experienced river paddlers only

LAUNCH INFO:

The Greenville Dam portage and access area is located at the intersection of Roosevelt, Smith, and Eighth Street in Norwich, CT. At first glance, this might not look like a public access area from the street. It is surrounded by chain link fence and the area contains a small utility building and a small gravel parking area. Looking closely at the fence, paddlers will see a sign advising that this is indeed a "public recreation area." This area is closed at sunset.

Even if the swing gate on the access road beyond the parking area is open and unlocked, I don't trust that it will be when I return. I have seen the gate to the dam's access road closed and locked during the day. I always park in the parking area outside that access road gate and I always bring along a kayak dolly when using this portage/launch area. I have dollied my kayak up the almost ¼ mile gravel dirt access road to the portage area and back when I wanted to paddle up river and the gate was closed/locked. I wouldn't advise doing that unless you're in excellent physical condition because it slopes uphill and in some cases it is washed out and bumpy.

FROM THE RIVER: The portage area will be river left before the buoys as paddlers approach the dam from up river. The condition of the portage area was poor when we last visited this site: the water at the portage area was full of sticks, branches, leaves and mud, and we got muddy using it.

Paddle at your own risk and discretion; only you can determine what is, or is not, safe and appropriate for you and your level of experience and condition. It is your responsibility to determine the legality, suitability, and safety of paddling at the destinations and paddling routes in this book. Read all applicable signs at the launch sites and be aware of boating regulations for each specific area before paddling. The author assumes no liability for accidents happening to, and/or injuries and/or damages sustained by readers and/or others who engage in the activities in this book. This book should not be a paddlers only source of information for the kayaking destinations in this book.

LAST PADDLED: 9/10/14

OUR EXPERIENCES:

There is a lot of history to be seen in the area above the Greenville dam, such as pieces of stone foundations and walls, the old Ponemah Mill, the old mill dam, and the facility at the mouth of the Quinebaug River. We also watched bald eagles, osprey, herons, ducks and the 6 swans that floated along with us for quite a while, allowing us to watch them eat and act as they would if we weren't among them.

The swans traveled with us for at least a mile and I suspect they might have previously been fed by humans. Unlike some panhandling birds that I've encountered, they were polite and kept the same boundaries for us as they did each another. What an excellent nature bonding experience. We watched fish jump with their entire bodies breaching the surface. It's not a wonder why the bald eagles and ospreys live there!

There were times when we escaped the sounds of civilization and then other times when we could hear traffic in the background, but the beauty was always there and it was a very relaxing trip. I'm not one for graffiti, however, one piece of art on a railroad bridge made me smile. I tried to envision the young person up there on the side of that bridge creating the repeating pattern, the different colors…and the expressions, not knowing that I'd paddle up there and admire it.

Most recently, we did this 6 mile round trip paddle from the Greenville Dam to the old Ponemah Mill/dam (up river) and back in about 5 hours; however, we felt as though we rushed the trip and didn't get to look around as much as we would have liked.

We did this trip in the fall when the water is much lower than in the springtime so the current was weaker and it was easier paddling up river; however, we did have to walk a very short distance near the mill dam, pulling our kayaks behind us through ankle to knee deep water along a beach like shoreline. Although it may be tempting, I DO NOT suggest walking through the shallower portions of this river due to the uneven river bottom and the functioning dams on this river which can release water and create rapid changes in water level. Paddling up river as we did in the low water, might not be possible in the spring when the water is higher and the current is stronger, or when significant amounts of water are being released from dams upriver.

NOTE: If you like grinders and you're paddling in this area, consider visiting Vocatura (Italian) Bakery at 695 Boswell Ave (Route 12) in Norwich, CT. Fresh baked rolls. Best grinders in the area.

NOTES:

HALLS POND

EASTFORD, CT

Halls Pond is the biggest little pond in Eastern Connecticut! It is only a little over 80 acres; but, it is one of the most beautiful and serene ponds I've ever paddled! It is the many islands and rock formations on this pond that give it a tranquil feeling and the illusion that it's bigger than it actually is. It is a nice fishing and birding location.

TYPE: Pond, Fishing, Bird Watching

LAUNCH INFO:

The boat launch is located on Halls Pond Road in Eastford, CT. From Route 198, take Halls Pond Road, and then watch for the launch area on the left. There are only a few parking spaces close to the launch area however, paddlers can unload at the water and park along the sides of the dirt entry road

LAST PADDLED: 8/26/14

OUR EXPERIENCES:

Even though I didn't make it out to Halls Pond this past season, this is one of my favorite places to hang out and unwind. I most enjoy locating feeding osprey that are perched high in the trees and diving into the water from one of the islands; I then access the opposite side of the same island, and sneak up behind the feeding bird to get a truly front row seat! No binoculars required!

The many little islands and their sandy docking areas make this very easy if paddlers are observant and quiet. I have spent a significant amount of time watching osprey dive, and catch and eat fish from this up close and personal perspective! If you've ever found yourself wondering where all the Canada geese go for the summer---well, they're on Halls Pond; too many to count and beautiful to watch! Awesome experience! From a bird watching perspective, the islands are awesome...and the fish even swim up to greet me. LOL! Of course I fed them, doesn't everyone?

NOTES:

HAMBURG COVE
CONNECTICUT RIVER

LYME, CT

Hamburg Cove is long, narrow, and winding with a variety of things to see, including a playful miniature replica of an old ship, and if one paddles far enough, a simple, yet charming, wooden dragon. This cove is lightly to moderately populated with sections of wooded areas. Many of the houses are tucked back among the trees, adding to the illusion that it's not as populated as it actually is. There are anchored motor boats and motor boat traffic coming to and from this cove.

Eagles, hawks, geese, ducks, cormorants, and deer can be found throughout the cove. *(See our experiences below.)*

TYPE: River Cove, Wildlife, Birding

LAUNCH INFO:

I have paddled Hamburg Cove by accessing it from northern launches on the Connecticut River, such as the Salmon River launch *(See page 187)* and during one of our river paddling campouts at Selden Island *(See page 189)*. However, I've been told that there is a an unofficial launch for Hamburg Cove at the intersections of Hamburg Road *(Route 156)* and Cove Road in Lyme, CT. I have not used this launch at the intersection of Hamburg Road and Cove Road so I cannot vouch for its existence or usability. There are also marinas nearby on the Connecticut River that could be used to access this cove.

LAST PADDLED: 8/27/15

OUR EXPERIENCES:

Recently, we saw a variety of wildlife including deer and several types of birds; the majority of them being viewed within the mouth of Hamburg Cove which faces Brockway Island *(See page 46)* on the Connecticut River. I really enjoyed the Cormorants with their out stretched wings, sunning themselves on docking buoys like cove sentinels. These birds somehow always make me chuckle!

During our last paddle at this location, we paddled up through the cove and to the right just before Cove Landing Marina, passing under the Cove Road bridge where it turns into Falls Brook. It became impossible to paddle further than the area immediately around the wooden dragon art lurking in the initial cove like area of the brook. We saw a large flock of geese in this same area and watched them for a bit. We headed back without seeing the remainder of the cove because it was getting late and we needed to reach our take-out river destination before dark.

NOTES:

HAMPTON RESERVOIR

HAMPTON, CT

Don't overlook Hampton Reservoir due to its size! Just shy of 90 acres, this pond unfolds. Paddling in and around the maze of swamp brush and mud patties, can present paddlers with the opportunity to see several beaver huts, an occasional muskrat, beaver, geese, ducks, turtles and deer.

Paddlers leave the canoe at home; bring the kayak and binoculars to spy on the wildlife while maneuvering throughout the narrow water trails of the swamp! Very early morning or late evening are best for viewing the wildlife.

TYPE: Reservoir, Pond, Wildlife/Bird Watching

LAUNCH INFO:

The boat launch is located on Kenyon Road in Hampton, CT. Watch for the boat launch sign on Rte 97 (at the junction of Kenyon Rd). There is no boat launch sign on Kenyon Road; the launch will be on the left about 1 1/2 miles from Route 97. Paddlers will first see a roadway with a gate across it--the boat launch will be the next dirt roadway on the left.

This is a nice launch; however, paddlers may find themselves shimmying their kayaks through shallow water and mud in order to get to open paddle able water.

LAST PADDLED: 2014

OUR EXPERIENCES:

During our 2014 visit, there were several large beaver huts that seemed to be uninhabited. My dog actually got off the kayak and walked on one of the larger huts like he thought he was going ashore. I didn't find any newly chewed wood added or around the beaver huts and no apparent food being stored under water near them so I couldn't be sure if beavers were still using them; but, I suspect, at least some were not in use.

I was disappointed by this until I found an area of new construction on the far side of the pond! The newly chewed wood stood out from quite some distance away, and as I paddled closer, I could see new construction underway and paths being created along the shoreline in that area.

Don't know what may have caused the decline of the beavers in this area; but, it was encouraging to still see at least some minimal activity on the opposite side of the pond.

NOTES:

HERON COVE TO EAGLEVILLE LAKE

WILLIMANTIC RIVER

TOLLAND, CT

(See photo page 132*)

This section of river requires knowledge of how to identify rocks in the stronger areas of current/rapids and then how to avoid those rocks while at the same time not becoming caught in the current and spun around or taken under dead trees hanging into the water. While the current and intro rapids are not great, the real danger is in not recognizing some of the bigger rocks within these conditions.

There are situations that could be tricky for paddlers who are only accustomed to flat water conditions. For example, some of the areas of stronger current are in winding areas of the river, and if paddlers don't know how to maneuver corners in these situations, they could easily be spun around and even dunked! According to NECKRA, the rapids experienced on this stretch of river are class I and II rapids. 1

There has been an annual sponsored river paddle race on this section of the river during the month of April. *See NECKRA reference page 97.*

TYPE: River, Seasonal access only

LAUNCH INFO:

Heron Cove Park boat launch is located on River Park Road in Tolland, CT. Enter the park, turn left and pass through the parking lot, and the launch will be just ahead beyond the sign. It has a very nice wood platform launch which requires paddlers enter kayaks from the dock.

The final destination for this trip is the Eagleville Pond boat launch which is located at the dam at 30 Pine Lake Drive in Coventry, CT. The Eagleville launch leaves a lot to be desired! It's steep with slippery rocks and it doesn't go into the water far enough. One of the paddlers that took this trip with us last spring, maneuvered some tricky paddling situations with great ease and then fell in the water getting out of his kayak at this end point. Be careful. I get in/out to the side of the launch or have someone steady the kayak if I do use it.

LAST PADDLED: 4/26/15

OUR EXPERIENCES:

I enjoy this down river trip very much. As one of my fellow paddlers recently said, it's varied conditions make for nice changes that paddlers don't experience within flat water situations. It's not a boring ho-hum trip; but, it would not be considered difficult by experienced river paddlers who regularly paddle in these conditions.

This 3+ hour trip from Heron Cove Park in Tolland, CT to Eagleville Lake in Coventry, CT is definitely an early spring event! In late April, the water was already low enough in some areas that our kayaks and one canoe scraped bottom in a few spots. While this section of the river has its low areas, it also has some deep areas; we met a young man scuba diving for lures and some fishermen taking advantage of a few of these deeper areas; however, nobody that we talked to had caught any fish. We didn't see much in the way of wildlife; however, the rusty railroad bridge and other bridges along the way added visual interest to this paddle.

On a few occasions, we found ourselves wondering which way to go when the river seemed to fork in two directions. We found that in these situations both led to the same destination. There are a few inlet areas that might look like alternate routes; but the water is pooling into those. When paddlers see moving water going two different ways, they can very likely go either way.

1. NECRA Reference: http://www.neckra.org/races/schedule/points-races

NOTES:

RIVER TIP FOR BEGINNERS

Just because someone may say that they have paddled a certain section of river, does not mean that it was a smart or safe thing to do. Please do your own research, scout all potential paddles, ask questions, wear a PFD and whistle. Beginners, please paddle with an experienced river paddler who has previously paddled that particular river. Utilizing these tips will increase your knowledge and confidence; and to an even greater extent, it could save your life. Experienced river paddlers, please, do not include inexperienced paddlers into situations where they are far exceeding their level of experience and understanding of the situation.

HOPEVILLE POND: PACHAUG RIVER ACCESS

GRISWOLD, CT

The Pachaug "River" is actually a collection of dammed ponds with little tail-like stretches of "river" attached to them. Unlike the local Quinebaug River, this river cannot be paddled for long uninterrupted distances due to the dams separating the ponds from other portions of the river. For this reason, these different sections of the Pachaug River will be presented under the pond to which the little river tail is attached.

Everything of interest is to the left of the Hopeville Pond launch and it gets more interesting as paddlers leave the pond and enter the Pachaug River. Going right after leaving this launch area will only bring paddlers past the main beach area, houses, a large mobile home park, a long shallow area of lily pads, and finally to the falls/dam area *(stay back)* immediately after the bridge. The falls/dam at this location is the same falls/dam at the end of the Ashland Pond river paddle *(Page 17)*. *No formal dam portage w/loose slippery rocks and tricky point of entry.*

Camping is also available at this site; however, leave the dog at home because dogs are not allowed.

TYPE: State Park, Camping, Rustic Pachaug River Access, Pond, Swimming

LAUNCH INFO:

The Hopeville Pond State Park boat launch is located in the campground area of the Hopeville Pond State Park on Hopeville Road *(near Route 201)* in Griswold, CT. This is a convenient launch for campers; but, not so much for paddlers who are not camping. Visiting paddlers need to drop kayaks off at the launch, then park behind the camp office, and walk back to the launch.

The launch is located within a small cove like area; so, paddlers should mark the entrance to the main body of water when leaving so that it will be easier to find it when they return. There is often a soda can hanging on a tree branch for this purpose. Please remove any additional markers when returning.

Paddlers can paddle up river to the Pachaug Pond water fall and return to this site when water level and current cooperate. Paddlers can also put-in at the launch near the intersection of Bitgood Road and Route 138 in Griswold, CT (parking for two vehicles without trailers--also additional parking at the church parking lot across the street) and paddle down to the Hopeville Pond launch. I suggest paddling up river from the Route 138 launch to the Pachaug Pond Falls and take a peek at the falls (5-10 minutes up and back). In my opinion, all the falls on the Pachaug River are worth a peek. *None of the falls/dams on this river have formal portages and all could be dangerous to portage.*

No dogs allowed in campground/launch area.

LAST PADDLED: 7/10/14

OUR EXPERIENCES:

We saw, and followed a large white catfish in the upper part of this section of river during our 2014 paddle from Hopeville Pond to the falls and back. There were trees to shimmy over and a few branches to wiggle under; but, nothing crazy hard. This is best paddled before the water level recedes later in the season; more and more downed trees breach the surface as the paddling season progresses and the water level recedes. We encountered two fishermen during our last paddle on this section of river.

HOWARD BROWN MEMORIAL PARK

NORWICH, CT

Where in Connecticut can one paddle on three rivers in one afternoon? In Norwich, of course! The Yantic River and the Shetucket River flow into the Thames River at the Howard Brown Memorial Park in Norwich, CT

This is an area rich with history; up the Yantic River is Indian Leap (Yantic Falls) with its many historic tales; at the mouth of the Shetucket River is the old rail road bridge and tunnel; down the Thames River, paddlers will find many old mills, old piers, remnants of the past, and even the metal hull of a ship *(river left)* grounded and rising above the water reminding all that it once was a magnificent ship *(Photo page 217)*. During winter months, paddlers may even see migrating Harbor Seals.

This section of the Thames River can be choppy at times. For example, the right combination of wind, tide, and release of water from the Greenville Dam on the Shetucket River can cause the water to be very choppy where the three rivers converge. At other times, the river conditions can be very smooth. Wind, weather, tide, release of water from the dam can quickly change conditions.

Both Poquetanuck Cove and Stoddard Cove are about 5 miles down river and are possible take-out locations for a down river trip. Both are accessed by paddling under a bridge along the Thames River. NOTE: the Stoddard Cove area at low tide can be so low that kayaks scrape bottom while attempting to access the launch area. At low tide, the Poquetanuck Cove southern launch will require a longer walk up a hill to the parking area with kayaks; but, is still very accessible at low tide *(See page 149)*. From a distance perspective only, there is no advantage to using one vs. the other because they are very close to one another.

Of course paddlers could paddle further down the Thames River to more distant take-outs, such as the Gold Star Memorial Bridge in New London *(See page 203)*; however, paddling conditions will be more tide like, and there will be more big boats to contend with the further one paddles down this river towards the shore. These conditions require prior knowledge of how to negotiate these types of boating situations and the rules and regulations involved, as well as, a solid knowledge of how to paddle in tidal river conditions.

CAUTION:

The Shetucket River has hydro-electric dams on it, and one located directly upriver from this location. When the dam releases extra water, the water below the dam can rise quickly and without warning. If paddlers are close to the dam, they should hear loud blasts before the water is released; if paddlers hear these blasts, they should immediately get themselves and their gear out of the water until the change in water level has occurred.

Paddlers should always have a whistle and please wear a PFD! The Shetucket River is not a place for beginners! Only well seasoned paddlers who have substantial river experience and direct and significant knowledge of this river should attempt to paddle the Shetucket River.

Paddle at your own risk and discretion; only you can determine what is, or is not, safe and appropriate for you and your level of experience and condition. It is your responsibility to determine the legality, suitability, and safety of paddling at the destinations and paddling routes in this book. Read all applicable signs at the launch sites and be aware of boating regulations for each specific area before paddling. The author assumes no liability for accidents happening to, and/or injuries and/or damages sustained by readers and/or others who engage in the activities in this book. The information in this book should not be a paddlers only source of information for these paddling destinations.

TYPE: Thames, Yantic & Shetucket River Boat Launch

LAUNCH INFO:

Howard T Brown Memorial Park is located at 100 Chelsea Harbor Drive in Norwich, CT. At times, the parking area at this park is full due to activities going on in the area and paddlers will need to drop off, park, and walk back. There is a parking garage within sight of the park.

LAST PADDLED: 1/26/16

OUR EXPERIENCES:

Most recently, we took advantage of an unseasonably warm January afternoon, to paddle from the Howard Brown Launch to Poquetanuck Cove *(See Poquetanuck Cove page 149)*. The highlight of this trip was watching a migrating Harbor Seal watching us in the water nearby! We enjoyed this curious animal very much.

We have paddled down the Thames River, up the Yantic River to Indian Leap and back, and up the Shetucket River and back on various occasions from this launch. This is considered a tidal area; however, it is far enough up river that this area doesn't experience the more significant effects one would expect to encounter further down the Thames River. That's not to say that the river isn't sometimes choppy! During our last paddle down the Thames, the wind was blowing opposite the tide and the water was very choppy in some parts of the river. I recommend this paddle to experienced tidal river paddlers who are also interested in local history.

SAFETY TIP FOR DOG OWNERS

If you paddle with a dog, consider including a laminated photo of your dog (preferably one of it on/in your kayak) in your first aid kit and another in a predominant location in your wallet or other item where rescuers may look for your vital information. On the photo, write, "DOG MAY BE ON BOARD." Also, put the dogs name and the name that you use to call the dog on the back along with your phone number, an alternate number, and the number of your dog's veterinarian. If something happens to you and you are not able to assist your dog or speak to rescuers, they will likely look in your wallet for your vital information. The photo of your kayaking dog in a prominent position in your wallet or first aid kit might be the only thing that alerts them to the idea that they should also look for a dog.

For more valuable kayaking with a dog information, check out my book, DOG PADDLING WITH TINY: A Guide To Kayaking With A Dog at KayakingCTwithLou.com.

INDIAN LEAP
(YANTIC FALLS)

NORWICH, CT

There are at least a couple of different folk stories surrounding Indian Leap; some involving Indian chiefs during a time of war, and others surrounding a young woman who allegedly died at the cliffs. Whether these tales are true, or they have been created and embellished over time, the cliffs and falls are well worth paddling up to see! Looking at the correct angle, paddlers may even see what looks like a face in the cliff wall *(See photo on page 2)*.

This paddle is best done late summer and fall because the water level is lower and the current less strong; however, the view of the falls is more spectacular with more water flowing over it in the early months of the paddling season. It is approximately a 1 ½ mile paddle upriver to the falls from the Howard Brown Launch.

NOTE: After paddling up this section of the Yantic River, and when facing the apartment building (old mill) , be sure to paddle all the way to that shoreline before turning left and then paddling to the area before the falls. This left turn isn't obvious until paddlers are right on top of it. Some paddlers hear the falls and turn too soon. If paddlers turn too soon, they will not be able to paddle directly into the area just before the falls. Stay back from the falls; there is a swirling current beneath the surface, that combined with the water coming over the falls, can flip a kayak and create a potentially dangerous situation.

There are also trails that lead up and around the falls area that can be accessed at Indian Leap Park in Norwich CT or by following the Heritage Trail path that starts at Howard Brown Memorial Park; the trail goes through wooded paths and streets before arriving at the upper falls location. Signs at the Howard Brown Park Launch area state, NO DOGS.

TYPE: River, Falls, Cliffs, Historical

LAUNCH INFO:

The launch for this up river paddle is at the Howard Brown Memorial Park at 100 Chelsea Harbor Drive in Norwich, CT. Nice formal launch; but, generally paddlers are not able to get parking spots in the immediate area of the launch during peak season and larger boats also use this ramp.

LAST PADDLED: 10/7/15

OUR EXPERIENCES:

I have paddled to Indian Leap three time in 2015. Paddlers who have experienced any part of the Yantic River, know that the river is generally more shallow in late summer and fall. This also means that the area before the Indian Leap Falls is likely to also be easier to approach with the generally calmer current coming from it.

On a previous 2015 paddle, it took us 5 ½ hours to paddle up to Indian Leap and back, and then down the Thames River to Traders Cove and back, then tying it all together with a little peek up the Shetucket River. I recommend this area to history buffs because it is rich in historical value.

Be aware that paddling too close to falls can be extremely dangerous; falls can look deceptively calm and inviting because the turbulence beneath the water is not always readily apparent to inexperienced paddlers. The turbulence and current at the base of any falls can have the potential to quickly roll a kayak and expose paddlers to unforeseen obstructions under the surface. Paddling too close to falls can be a potentially dangerous situation!

NOTES:

Occum Dam on the Shetucket River.
(See page 196)

LANTERN HILL POND

LEDYARD, CT

Lantern Hill Pond is only **23 acres** and is primarily a fishing spot. One can pretty much see it all without going out in a kayak; however, I had a very neat up close and personal with a muskrat while paddling on this pond *(See our experience below)*.

Lantern Hill (cliff area) is a popular hiking spot nearby. The cliff can be seen rising above the backside of the small pond and the trail can be accessed on Wintechog Hill Road in Ledyard, CT. *See reference at end of entry for more details about this hiking experience.*

TYPE: Pond, Fishing, Hiking at Lantern Hill (cliff) nearby

LAUNCH INFO:

The launch is located on Lantern Hill Road in Ledyard, CT. It has a very nice parking area and launch for a 23 acre pond!

Paddlers and those wishing to view the pond and the facing cliffs can park in the upper parking area and walk down the path or take the very short launch road to the water's edge.

LAST PADDLED: 8/27/14

OUR EXPERIENCES:

Me being me, I had to put my kayak onto this tiny **23 acre** pond and I was immediately rewarded for my effort! While pushing off from the launch area, I turned to my right and found myself face to face with a muskrat. I recall saying something like, "Oh shit, a muskrat," while quickly fumbling to get settled and locate my camera! LOL! I really need to practice keeping my excitement to myself!

By the time I was ready to snap a photo of the water rat, it had, ever so casually, entered the water and was slowly swimming away. Silly human! I paddled out to the middle of the pond and watched him with my binoculars as I ate an orange from my pack. The muskrat went about his business as if I wasn't there.

The fishermen that I encountered, leaving as I was arriving, said they caught a small bass.

HIKING REFERENCE:
http://www.mdc.net/~dbrier/yawgoog/trails/narragansett.html

NOTES:

LIEUTENANT RIVER

OLD LYME, CT

Paddling the Lieutenant River had been on my to-do paddle list ever since I visited the Florence Griswold Museum in Old Lyme, CT. I'm not the kind of person who generally hangs out in art museums; however, when I learned that the museum *(located on the shore of the Lieutenant River)* was once an art colony, I had to go. After viewing the beautiful paintings and drawings of the river, I found myself walking in the snow along the river's edge, vowing to return and paddle this river!

Perspective is everything! I paddled the Lieutenant River with a hope of being inspired by whatever it was that inspired those artists! Sadly, I think our modern world has stolen at least some of this river's inspiring charm. We heard highway traffic to varying degrees throughout most of the trip and passed under a few bridges where it was even louder. There are a variety of birds to be seen; however, overall, I would recommend other locations in the area before this one *(See next entry)*.

TYPE: Tidal River, Birding

LAUNCH INFO:

The Lieutenant River boat launch is located by a bridge on Route 156 *(Shore Road)* near Ferry Road in Old Lyme. Turn right from the stop sign at Ferry Road and the launch will be on the left after the bridge on Route 156.

LAST PADDLED: 7/30/15

OUR EXPERIENCES:

We saw several heron, swans with little ones, egrets *(large and small)*, osprey and osprey nests, and many other smaller birds. Two paddlers told us about a spot where we might see a bald eagle; but, we didn't see it. The birds that we did encounter didn't seem to mind and allowed us to paddle in close.

We paddled up river with the incoming tide and paddled back at slack tide. We went up the two feeder rivers *(as far as was possible)* and back as well. To be completely honest, I enjoyed paddling on the feeder Millbrook River more so than the Lieutenant River. Millbrook River was narrow and it had big rocks, beaver dams, and graffiti under the Sill Lane bridge that declared we should preserve art in Old Lyme!

After returning to the launch, we took a break and then paddled down to the point where the Lieutenant River empties out into the Connecticut River. The railroad draw bridge *(Photo page 10)* is quite impressive. It's the same Connecticut River draw bridge that can be seen while paddling around Great Island.

While I wasn't all that impressed with the Lieutenant River, I was impressed with the Connecticut River By Pass paddle between the Lieutenant River and Great Island *(see next entry)*.

NOTES:

LIEUTENANT RIVER TO GREAT ISLAND

CONNECTICUT RIVER BY-PASS PADDLE

LYME, CT

This trip is interesting from a birding perspective and it also has a few points of interest, including the Great Island Estuary *(page 79)*, the lighthouse *(cover photo)*, and the draw bridge *(See photo page 10)*.

The Connecticut River by-pass paddle from the Lieutenant River to the back side of Marvin Island and on to the Great Island launch is an awesome birding paddle; but, also a way to avoid paddling against the tide on the Connecticut River for a nice round trip paddle, starting and ending at either of the two launches involved. There are a few ways to use this paddle pass-through behind Marvin Island and Great Island. Paddlers can paddle with the tide up or down that section of the Connecticut River and then form a loop by going down or up the back passage behind the two islands, and thereby avoiding paddling against the tide on the Connecticut River. Paddlers could also paddle both ways on the back passage behind Marvin Island and Great Island and avoid paddling on the Connecticut River all together, starting at one launch and ending at the other, or by returning to the same launch.

I recommend ending at the Great Island Launch over the Lieutenant River Launch because paddlers will have more options if they find that they have additional time. For example, paddlers could go up the Black Hall River (short distance at low tide) or paddle around Great Island and stop at one of the sandy beaches (tide can affect access). The Great

Island boat launch is near the mouth of the Connecticut River and also provides coastal access to the sound. Low tide can affect access to some areas involved in this back passage. *(Great Island photo page 80)*

TYPE: Tidal River, Birding

LAUNCH INFO:

The Great Island launch is located at 99 Smith Neck Road (off Rte 156), in Old Lyme, CT and is 500' from Great Island. Nice parking area, turning area, and ramp. In addition to close and almost immediate access to Great Island Wildlife Preserve, this launch also provides an access point for Long Island Sound, places like the Black Hall River, and the back entrance to the Lieutenant River discussed above.

The Lieutenant River launch is located by a bridge on Route 156 (Shore Road) near Ferry Road in Old Lyme. Turn right from the stop sign at Ferry Road and the launch will be on the left after the bridge on Route 156.

LAST PADDLED: 9/9/15

OUR EXPERIENCES:

On our most recent paddle, we paddled left from the Great Island Launch to the mouth of the Connecticut River, then across the Connecticut River to the Light House, where we ate lunch and watched boats on the less populated beach to the north *(cover photo)*. When high tide started to really kick in, we decided to ride the current up to the draw bridge *(photo page 10)*. The tide-assist was great fun and required very little paddling.

We didn't want to paddle back against that strong current so we ducked into the mouth of the Lieutenant River *(right side of the draw bridge when paddling up river)*, then took the first right and meandered our way down to the back side of Marvin Island and on to the back side of Great Island, enjoying a wide variety of birds along the way. This back way to the Great Island Launch is a very nice birding experience!

If paddlers enter the mouth of the Lieutenant River to do this (as we did), and they arrive at the Lieutenant River Launch at the bridge, then they've gone too far. A GPS can assist paddlers in finding this access point. as well as, assist paddlers as they meander through the channels, peninsulas, grasses, and mini islands involved in this paddle pass-through.

Earlier this season, I paddled around Great Island and enjoyed watching osprey feeding their young at the many nesting platforms located on, and in the area of, Great Island. We also got out and spent time on the long stretch of beach located on the Connecticut River side of Great Island. Tide will affect access. Paddlers will likely see gulls and pipers, as we did, on the Connecticut River side of the island as well.

Due to the immediate access to the Sound, I recommend using a skirted sea kayak--especially if there is wind or other conditions that would increase waves and current. *Paddle at your own risk and discretion; only you can determine what is, or is not, safe and appropriate for you and your level of experience and condition.*

NOTES:

WINTER PADDLING
SAFETY TIP

A dry suit can be an expensive purchase; however, it can save a paddler's life if their kayak flips or they fall into water that is cold enough to cause hypothermia. A dry suit can have a nice wind breaking effect while paddling; however, it <u>WILL NOT</u> keep a paddler warm after falling into frigid water! It will keep a paddler dry if/when they fall in and, therefore, make the warm up process quicker and more efficient when the paddler gets out of the frigid water. Arriving on dry land or back in the kayak dry is a huge advantage over the person who is soaking wet! *See photo back flap.*

LONG POND

LEDYARD, CT

Long Pond is 109 acres with a posted and enforced speed limit of no more than 5 miles an hour so paddlers shouldn't have to deal with high speed boats or water skiing. The shores of this pond are moderately to heavily populated in some areas and we found many of the residents on, and around, the water even on a week day afternoon. There is very little shade in many areas of this pond during the middle of the day.

Paddling through a tunnel under Lantern Hill Road brings paddlers to the smaller but more private section of the pond. This access is on the same side as the boat launch, but closer to the opposite end of the pond. Cormorants, swans, heron, and various ducks can be seen here.

TYPE: Pond, Bird Watching

LAUNCH INFO:

The boat launch is cement plank and is located on the Route 214 end of Lantern Hill Road in Ledyard, CT. Paddlers coming from the Route 214 end of Lantern Hill Road, will pass Lantern Hill Pond on the left; but, Lantern Hill Pond is only 23 acres. Continuing past Lantern Hill Pond, paddlers will see the boat launch sign for Long Pond on the right. There is ample parking and an easily accessible ramp and a turning area suitable for car top and trailers.

LAST PADDLED: 8/27/14

OUR EXPERIENCES:

Paddling on Long Pond is comparable to walking down Main Street in one's home town. We were engaged in conversation by several friendly residents who initiated conversation. We also spoke with a couple of fishermen, who told us no fish had been caught-yet! We were reminded of the five mile an hour speed limit when speaking with some of the residents--this caused me to chuckle because, after all, we were paddling in kayaks! I would guess that the 5 mph speed limit is strictly enforced.

Watching an immature heron catch and feed on dragonflies was the most remarkable thing I witnessed while paddling on this pond. We also saw swans, ducks, and cormorants. The two cormorants that kept reappearing near us seemed to toy with us, and I suspect they are fed by locals and perhaps other paddlers? Due to their playful and trusting nature, I was able to get some nice photos of them.

NOTES:

LORD COVE: CONNECTICUT RIVER

LYME, CT

Lord Cove is like a corn maze on water, with many inlets that loop around and come back or connect to other water ways, and some that abruptly end-- wide, narrow, deep, and shallow, it's all there. Tide definitely affects passage in at least some of these waterways.

The northern side of Goose Island forms the lower boundary of Lord Cove and the main body of Goose Island forms the boundary of Lord Creek. Paddlers entering at the Pilgrim Landing Launch, should stay right and follow the shoreline through Lord Creek and into Lord Cove.

CAUTION: Hunting takes place in the lower area near Goose Island during the proper season. Paddlers can easily identify the area by the duck blinds belonging to a local gun club.

TYPE: Brackish Tidal Cove. Bird Watching

LAUNCH INFO:

The Pilgrim Landing Launch is located on Pilgrim Landing Road off Route 156 in Old Lyme, CT; watch for this road on the left when coming from Route 95 or the Lieutenant River Launch. Pilgrim Landing has about 8 parking spaces if everyone parks close together.

At the Pilgrim Landing Launch, paddlers will see Calves Island out and slightly to the left with its large sandy beach and Baldwin Bridge towering in the distance beyond it. Goose Island can be seen slightly to the right; this is where the swallows swarm at sunset in the fall *(See swarming of the swallows page 201)*. Pilgrims Landing is a nice launch for kayaks and canoes because there is less motor boat traffic than at the Baldwin Bridge Launch which is located further down river beyond Calves Island.

Baldwin Bridge Launch: If for some reason, the Pilgrim Landing parking area is full, paddlers can launch at the launch/parking area at the Baldwin Bridge boat launch and paddle up; but, that paddle will take about a half hour and paddlers will likely encounter more motor boat traffic than launching at the Pilgrim Landing Launch. Baldwin Bridge Launch is a DEEP boat launch area and is located at 220 Ferry Road in Old Saybrook, CT.

LAST PADDLED: 9/16/15

OUR EXPERIENCES:

We were in the area to watch the migratory end of day swallow swarm around Goose Island *(See swarming of the swallows page 201)*. We launched from the Pilgrim Landing Launch and spent a few hours paddling Lord Cove while we waited for the sun to sink lower in the sky. We encountered a couple of fishermen and saw swans, geese, heron, osprey, ducks, and egrets during our paddle. Choosing a nice shady spot to eat, we watched seven swans lazily feeding just ahead of us.

This beautiful and relaxing paddle combined with the birds and the varied twists and turns held my attention and piqued my curiosity. I will definitely go back to explore this cove more when I can spend the day!

NOTES:

MASHAPAUG LAKE

UNION, CT

This 287 acre lake, Breakneck Pond, and Bigelow Hollow Pond are located within Bigelow State Park in Union CT. The lake is open year round and has a 10 mph speed limit on the water. There are picnicking and swimming areas, hiking trails, and seasonal chemical toilets at this park. Some shoreline areas are populated and all the islands on the lake are private do-not enter areas.

There is a very small parking area for the large number of seasonal weekend visitors to this lake. Unloading kayaks and equipment, then driving back down the access road, parking and walking back might be an issue for people with small children, health issues, dogs, or vehicles pulling trailers.

There is a small weekend access fee to this park.

TYPE: Lake, State Park, Swimming, Hiking, Picnicking, Boating

LAUNCH INFO:

The launch is located at the end of the main access road through the park. The parking area for this launch is small and sometimes congested for the number of boaters visiting this site on summer weekends! Paddlers often have to unload, drive back down the entry road, park, and walk back to the launch. It has a very nice launch after addressing the parking issues!

LAST PADDLED: 8/10/14

OUR EXPERIENCES:

It is truly a nice place for a family outing; however, I would not rate it as a top pick for a kayaking only trip. My return to Mashapaug Lake brought back many happy memories of family barbecues, swimming, fishing and boating with my Dad. The sounds of laughter, chatting, music, and the smell of barbecue filled the air, causing me to smile and fill with expectation before I even exited our truck!

This lake has some beautiful tall trees surrounding some of it; but, beautiful trees kept my attention for only a short time. I was ready to go before having paddled around the entire lake and I usually enjoy paddling all day at other more interesting locations. There were generally several boaters within our field of vision at all times, lessening only as we got further from the launch area and we didn't see much wildlife or birds.

I suggest that paddlers make a day of it, and include some picnicking, swimming, and hiking...and of course, a paddle on Bigelow Hollow Pond near the entrance of the park. *(See Bigelow Hollow Pond 39).*

NOTES:

MASON ISLAND

MYSTIC, CT

Mason Island and the surrounding area is a pleasant paddling experience; however, it is at the mouth of the Mystic River facing open water. This is not a place for novice paddlers and recreational kayaks. Only experienced coastal river paddlers with sea kayaks should venture into this area.

Paddlers can choose to paddle around the entirety of Mason Island, including Enders Island, or skip paddling around Enders Island by paddling under the bridge that connects it to Mason Island. On the opposite side of Mason Island, paddlers will find Dodges Island and Andrews Island which can also be paddled around. River right of Mason Island is Six Penny Island which is a nature preserve. Ram Island is located in open water South West of Mason Point and South East of Morgan Point.

Paddle at your own risk and discretion; only you can determine what is, or is not, safe and appropriate for you and your level of experience and condition. It is your responsibility to determine the legality, suitability, and safety of paddling at the destinations and paddling routes in this book. Read all applicable signs at the launch sites and be aware of boating regulations for each specific area before paddling. The author assumes no liability for accidents happening to, and/or injuries and/or damages sustained by readers and/or others who engage in the activities in this book. This book should not be paddlers only source of information for paddling destinations in this book.

TYPE: Island, Mouth of Mystic River

LAUNCH INFO:

There are a few launches available to paddle around Mason Island and the surrounding area; my favorite being the public Beebe Cove Launch located behind the Noank Recreational Department on Spicer Road in Noank, CT. Mystic Harbor and the area surrounding Mason Island can be accessed by paddling right from the Beebe Cove Launch, passing under the railroad bridge, and staying left while paddling out past the anchored boats in that area, paddlers will see Mason Island slightly to the left in front of them

LAST PADDLED: Summer 2015 (3x)

OUR EXPERIENCES:

This area is abundant with beautiful and interesting places to paddle and explore. I particularly like paddling around Enders Island which is connected to Mason Island by a bridge. The view of the privately owned retreat on Enders Island is partially blocked by the sea wall; however, at the far end of the sea wall, paddlers can catch a glimpse of some of the retreat's beautiful flower and vegetable gardens, and stone buildings. Caution: the water facing this sea wall can be rough paddling at times.

I have on occasion, had coffee and cake under the pergola in one of the flower gardens at the privately owned retreat on Enders Island. The view is breathtaking as is a summer walk through the garden paths.

I feel as though I'm on a mini vacation when watching the sail boats and birds, and enjoying the coastal atmosphere surrounding Ram Island. I've spent entire afternoons hanging out there. In fact, our first paddle to the Ram Island area was with the intention of checking out

Ram Island and then paddling on to Enders Island; however, we got caught up in watching the sail boats, birds, and the sparkle of the sun on the water, and we never made it to Enders Island that day.

NOTES:

Foggy morning on Middle Reservoir
(See facing page)

MIDDLE RESERVOIR

EAST KILLINGLY, CT

Middle Reservoir can be a good wildlife paddle, revealing several different birds and small animals in the early and late hours of the day; however, it is very weedy. There is a campground located along one section of it, but the remainder of the pond is conducive to water birds and other wildlife.

Paddlers will get some exercise if they choose to paddle on this pond due to the over growth of vegetation. Bring the bug spray because around sunset the mosquitoes can be brutal!

Caution: There is a tiny falls just before the Route 101 bridge; beyond the falls, and under the bridge, is Bog Meadow Reservoir *(See page 45)*. Please DO NOT try to run the falls. It looks small; however, even low falls can have serious turbulence and unseen obstacles and obstructions beneath the water. Paddlers who get turned under at a falls, often encounter objects related to the construction and support of the dam that can also cause injury as they are swirled about by the churning water. Stay back from the falls even though it might look harmless!

TYPE: Pond, Fishing, Bird/Wildlife Watching, Summer Campground RV Park

LAUNCH INFO:

Middle Reservoir is one of the five reservoirs clustered together in Eastern CT. It is located on Pond Road across from Alvia Chase Reservoir (off Rte 101) in East Killingly CT. Entering Pond Road from

Rte 101, Middle Reservoir will be on the left and Alvia Chase Reservoir on the right. Killingly Pond and Eddy Pray Reservoir are located further up the road. Paddlers will likely have some difficulty locating Eddy Pray Reservoir unless they have previously paddled there *(See page 61)*.

CAMPGROUND (RV PARK): Hide Away Cove, 1060 North Road, Dayville, CT. *I have never stayed at this location.*

LAST PADDLED: Summer 2014

OUR EXPERIENCES:

Paddlers will need a purpose before venturing out on Middle Reservoir, because without one, they will get frustrated and quickly move onto something easier to paddle. I've fished at this location growing up, and I have more recently done some bird and wildlife watching and photography at this location.

This can be an awesome wildlife paddle on a foggy morning just before sunrise. In fact, I won't show up to paddle at this location unless it is a foggy morning or a warm evening because I'm there to see the animals and birds. Bring your camera! I have taken some great wildlife and bird shots here.

The biggest deterrent is the mosquitoes which show up as soon as the sun starts to go down and the animals start to come out! The number of mosquitoes at this location after sunset is sometimes insane! No kidding!

NOTES:

MOOSUP RIVER

STERLING, CT

Several areas of the Moosup River are generally not paddleable due to low water and other access issues; some are not even paddleable with a decent spring thaw. In the following area of this river, paddlers can paddle up river and back to the same launch.

I would not put this section of the Moosup River on the CT tourist must see list; however, I would suggest it to local fishermen and local paddlers who might be tired of paddling all the same usual places in this area. At the start of this trip, paddlers will quickly find a trailer park, a few cute cottages, and also some run down buildings and trailers that do not look like they've been inhabited in quite a while; however, after paddling through this initial section, this part of the Moosup River rather quickly turns into an opportunity to feel like the paddler has been swept away from it all; no sounds of traffic, buildings, or other distractions.

This section of the Moosup River is narrow and generally slow; however, the current gets stronger further up river. The main dangers on this river are the fallen trees and log/tree jams. In some cases there are large trees that have fallen on top of other large fallen trees. This is a hazard that should not be over looked or minimized!

How far a paddler can go up river will depend upon the current, water level, and the strength and ability of the paddler to paddle the current as it increases further up river. There is some amount of rock dodging with more rocks appearing close to the surface later in the season when the water is lower; however, the rock dodging is not usually a serious issue for experienced river paddlers. Due to the slow meandering flow of this river, a watchful person can usually see them in time to avoid them.

TYPE: River

LAUNCH INFO:

The boat launch is located on the section of river adjacent the Sterling school on Rte 14A in Sterling CT. Paddlers will see the short dirt entry to the launch area on the right after entering the school parking lot. This dirt entry sometimes has very large pot holes in it; so, drive slowly and cautiously when entering this area. Once in the water, river access is to the left. Stay back from the bridge/falls to the right!

NOTE-DANGER/HAZARD: When entering the water at the launch area near the school, paddlers will see a bridge in the distance to their right, and should avoid going near that bridge with kayaks or other boats. There is a dam/water fall immediately after the bridge and this spillway is not buoyed/roped off as is the case in some other falls in the area. The drop is significant! Going left from the launch area will start the paddlers' journey up river.

LAST PADDLED: 5/10/15

OUR EXPERIENCES:

Most recently, we paddled up river for almost three hours, pausing occasionally to fish before turning back, and did not reach a point where we could not go on. However, there were some very shallow sections, so paddlers may not be able to paddle as far as we did later in the season when the water levels recede. Conversely, the higher spring water levels and swifter current can hinder progress in the early spring.

On our most recent trip, I stopped to watch a muskrat collecting food while my friends fished. It occasionally looked right at me; but, seemed OK with the whole thing as long as I kept my distance and was quiet. There was no, "Oh look there's a human;" just a casual glance every once and again to be sure I was still abiding by our unspoken agreement to stay outside one another's personal space. Besides this one encounter, I have not seen anything remarkable regarding birds and wildlife on this section of the river.

I have been told that trout, bass, and pickerel can be caught in this section of the Moosup River. The river conditions vary from deep to very shallow.

NOTES:

Willimantic River *(See page 95)*

MYSTIC RIVER
STATE BOAT LAUNCH

LOCATION

Mystic Seaport, the draw bridges, and the ice cream shop by the draw bridge are the highlights of the Mystic River paddle. The scheduled openings of the main draw bridge allow large boats to pass, while at the same time, allowing paddlers to view this bridge in action from the water. In the warmer months, this area is busy with activity and takes on a more touristy atmosphere.

There are advantages and disadvantages to paddling this river during the off season. In the off season, paddlers typically have the river to themselves, while in the warmer months, this area has a lot of boat traffic and anchored boats in the harbor. Places like Six Penny Island and Mason Island will appear to be more visually open and accessible because the surrounding water will not be covered with anchored boats. Occasionally migrating Harbor Seals can be seen wintering in this area as well. One disadvantage to paddling in the off season is that there are no scheduled openings of the draw bridges.

TYPE: Tidal River

LAUNCH INFO:

Put-in launch is at the Mystic State Boat Launch on River Road just north of Route 95. There is plenty of parking in the gravel pull-off area; however the launch is a washed out moderate slope, leveling off at the water. Easy water entry after maneuvering the uneven slope to the river.

Alternate put-in is located at the intersection of Bay Street and Holmes in Stonington, CT. It has a smaller paved launch; however, there is no on site parking.

Take-out is at the Beebe Cove Launch located behind the Noank Recreational Center on Spicer Road in Noank, CT.

LAST PADDLED: 2/1/16

OUR EXPERIENCES:

Most recently, we paddled from the Mystic River State Boat Launch to Beebe Cove in the off-season and were rewarded with seeing a migrating Harbor Seal and having the river virtually to ourselves! We took advantage of the unusually mild winter weather and paddled around all the ships at Mystic Seaport and briefly watched repairs being done to some of the great ships located there.

We paddled down around Mason Island, briefly stopping at Six Penny Island to collect shells before reaching our final destination. The Mystic Seaport experience and seeing the Harbor Seal was truly the highlights of this particular trip! Note: I wore a dry suit and took other cold weather paddling precautions for this winter paddle.

In the summer months we enjoy ice cream at the shop near the main draw bridge; this shop is literally right at the draw bridge.

The nice thing about this paddle is seeing things from a different perspective. Seeing the ships at Mystic Seaport and seeing the draw bridges from the water is very different than viewing them from the shore! I am always in awe of the main draw bridge every time I see it open. Of course, witnessing the draw bridge opening would be most likely accomplished during a summer paddle when there are scheduled openings of the main bridge and the railroad bridge.

NOTES:

Cecil & Lou's dog, Tiny, on the Moosup River
(See page 129)

OLD KILLINGLY POND

EAST KILLINGLY, CT

Old Killingly Pond, sometimes referred to as Killingly Pond or Killingly Reservoir, is one of 5 reservoirs clustered together in East Killingly, CT. It is spring fed, and so it is generally colder than other ponds in the area; this condition helps to resist over growth of algae and other green plants found in other ponds in the immediate area. As a result, the water is generally very clear in most areas of the pond.

Old Killingly Pond is a typical sit-in-spin pond with only a couple of interesting, but, very small inlet areas in the back left section and a very tiny island to the front right section of the pond. It is sparsely populated and pretty much looks the same all the way around it. I would not recommend driving out to do this particular pond if paddlers are looking for wildlife and interesting scenery; however, some nice bass have been taken from this pond! All of the other four East Killingly Reservoirs are more conducive to wildlife.

TYPE: Pond, Bass Fishing

LAUNCH INFO:

The launch is located on Pond Road in East Killingly, CT. Turn onto Pond Road from Route 101, pass Middle Reservoir (left) and Alvia Chase Reservoir (right), and Old Killingly Pond will be the next body of water on the right. The launch is to the left of the chain link fence. There is only limited off-road parking and sometimes finding a place to park can be an issue.

LAST PADDLED: 7/30/14

OUR EXPERIENCES:

During our last paddle at this location, we found ourselves looking into the water as much as we were looking around because we could see fish very clearly in the shallower parts of the pond. We even saw a few bass. A downed tree floating vertically beneath the water, also gave us a clear and very remarkable view of the depth of some areas of this pond.

I grew up in this area and have spent many hours on this pond and the other four reservoirs in the immediate area. I've seen some nice bass and large bullhead caught here!

NOTES:

PACHAUG POND

GRISWOLD, CT

This 841 acre pond is nice because there can be several boats out on the pond without everyone being on top of one another. I've been out on this pond and seen a dozen or more boaters without ever coming close enough to chat with any of them! On Pachaug Pond, there can be privacy in numbers!

There is often considerably more motorized water activities in the evenings during the boating season. As late afternoon and evening approach the speed boats, jet skis, and water skiers generally come out. So, paddlers who want privacy to fish or view wildlife will find the best opportunities during the early morning hours on a week day.

Much of Pachaug Pond is populated, and in some places heavily populated; but there are also some inlet areas that are good for fishing and for watching birds and other wildlife early in the morning. Muskrat, deer, owl, heron, ducks, geese, and other birds can be seen during the very early morning hours of the day on this pond.

TYPE: Pond, Fishing, Bird/Wildlife Watching

LAUNCH INFO:

The cement boat ramp is located on the north shore of the pond near the falls at 945 Voluntown Road (Rte 138), Griswold, CT. There is ample parking; but, there is a short walk from the parking area to the ramp which requires dropping off, parking, and walking back *(the walk would be equitable to walking to a parking lot located across a street).*

LAST PADDLED: 7/17/14

OUR EXPERIENCES:

The first time I paddled from this launch area, I thought, wow, this is going to be a kayaking tour of water-front homes and properties; but, I was pleasantly surprised! Much of Pachaug Pond is populated, and in some places, heavily populated; however, there are also some inlet areas with wildlife activity and I've been told fishing is good in these inlet areas as well.

During our most recent paddle at this location, we were on the pond from sunrise to about 6:15 pm on a weekday and paddled 12.8 miles without exploring the entire pond! We were there to see the sunrise, and later joined by a friend; when she left, we were joined by two other friends who paddled with us for a few hours. In the early morning hours we saw an owl, muskrat, ducks, a feeding heron, and another duck size water bird with a long beak and legs that we could not identify. We also saw pink water lilies--a change from the usual yellow and white. I've seen these pink lilies in Pineville on the Five Mile River as well.

I got some nice fog photos of a long wooden dock that was broken and falling into the water, as well as, some nice shots of an owl and heron at sunrise.

PACKER POND

PLAINFIELD, CT

Sometimes referred to as Mill Brook Pond, this pond is long and narrow, and continues further than can be seen from the informal launch. Beyond the main body of water is a short river like entry with maze like water ways between the cattails and other grasses; this wider section quickly narrows into a brook.

This is a fishing spot that gets a lot of visitors; I even saw someone ice fishing in an ice shack at this location on Valentines Day 2015. *Note: there is current flowing through this pond to a dam/falls; so the ice may be thinner than might be expected.*

There is much to be seen in, and around, this pond in the early morning and late evening hours. I have seen baby deer, muskrats, rabbits, and fox along the shoreline in pre-dawn and sunrise hours of the day. There are swans, ducks, and geese on the pond. The geese aren't usually as outwardly visible to visitors during the summer months; however, in the spring and fall they can be seen in nearby corn fields and floating about on Packer Pond. There are duck houses posted in the back section to encourage ducks into the area.

The pond flows over an unmarked spillway at the railroad bridge. Stay back from the dam/falls and the current leading up to the dam/falls. There are no markers indicating the presence of a dam/falls area and the drop is significant with shallow water and rocks at the base of it!

TYPE: Pond, Fishing, Birding/Wildlife Watching

LAUNCH INFO:

No boat launch; we pretty much put in the water where fishermen have worn out dirt areas along the water's edge (near the railroad tracks) on Mill Brook Road in Plainfield, CT. The steep embankment to the water might be tricky for someone new to kayaking. I've also put in along the side of this pond; however, plan on getting wet trying that! I don't know who owns this pond, so paddle here at your own risk and discretion; it is visited regularly by many locals who are fishing.

LAST PADDLED: Summer 2014

OUR EXPERIENCES:

I live very close to this location; so, I sometimes paddle here when I feel like paddling and there isn't enough time to go farther. I once drove by it on my way home from work, went home and got my kayak, and returned to paddle in the fog at sunrise. I enjoy paddling among the maze of cattails and tall grasses in search of the swans and other wildlife at the far end of this pond. The swans can be quite elusive; sometimes, if I didn't know they were there, I would believe none existed on the pond. Every year, we watch young swans grow into beautiful adults.

This pond is too small to travel any distance to fish or paddle here; however, if fishing or bird watching in the area, it might be worth a look.

NOTES:

PAWCATUCK RIVER: POTTER HILL DAM

ASHAWAY, RI (CT/RI RIVER BORDER)

This section of the Pawcatuck River runs along the Connecticut/Rhode Island border beginning just a short distance below the Potter Hill Dam. In general, the Pawcatuck River offers a variety of experiences. While much of it is flat water, it does have areas of white water, and the entire river is speckled with historical value, including remains of old mills, older homes, bridges, and even the dams themselves. Remains of an old mill can be viewed from the lower launch at this location.

TYPE: River, Historical

LAUNCH INFO:

The lower launch:

The launch to go down river is located at the intersection of Laurel Street and Maxson Street in Ashaway, Rhode Island. There is a dirt pull off area in which to park. We easily fit 3 trucks with room for another when we parked straight in towards the water. Paddlers should look for the path down to the river otherwise they will find themselves stumbling down through loose dirt and rocks to get there. Facing the water and the old mill beyond it, the path down to the water is to the right of the more obvious washed out area of sand, dirt, and rocks.

I was told, and I have read, that the White Rock Dam has been removed down river; so, I don't know what may or may not have changed in doing a down river trip from this launch. It is on our paddling agenda for the upcoming season.

The portage/launch to paddle up river is located just above the dam at the Elora Whitely Preserve next to the bridge on Potter Hill Road. This launch could also be used to portage the Potter Hill Dam by also utilizing the lower launch, to paddle up river and back to the same launch, or as a take-out when paddling down the Pawcatuck River from another RI put-in. There is literally only parking for one roadside vehicle due to a fire hydrant; we unloaded and parked around the corner at the lower launch area, leaving one vehicle at this site.

It is a rustic launch; however, paddlers will not find it difficult to use if they are dressed so that they can step into the water. Paddle right from the launch; the dam is on the left just beyond the bridge. There have been boating fatalities at the Potter Hill Dam so please stay back from the dam and fish ladder.

LAST PADDLED: 12/8/15

OUR EXPERIENCES:

We paddled up river from the dam. Shortly after beginning this up-river paddle, we found it necessary to stay right at the dead tree (center island); paddlers will quickly come to a swampy end if they go left instead of staying right. Paddlers who are following a map or GPS, will see islands that are in reality quite swampy and over grown on one side or the other. After the dead tree, the other swampy dead ends are a bit more obvious.

We paddled upriver a short distance beyond the Nooseneck Hill Road

Bridge and paddled 4.5 miles round trip. It was 45 degrees and spitting rain when we arrived on this December afternoon; so, we didn't encounter much wildlife. However, we did see some ducks and signs of beaver activity in this area. I would expect to see more wildlife in this area on a warmer day and with no threat of cold December rain in the forecast.

This was a very relaxing paddle; for those paddlers who are familiar with paddling the Butts Bridge area of the Quinebaug River in Canterbury, CT--this paddle is very similar but with a few more houses.

NOTES:

PADDLING SAFETY TIP

Personal Floatation Devices (PFDs) have become a really hot topic for some paddlers! I'm not going lecture or tell you that paddlers should wear a PFD. I will leave that to the boating regulations which clearly state when a PFD should be worn.

However, I will give you a few things to consider. I hear numerous excuses for not wearing a PFD, ranging from nobody is going to tell me what to do; I'm a great swimmer so I don't need one; it makes me hot, or it wrinkles my clothes. I'm only going to ask one question. Are you a great swimmer with a broken arm or leg, or a head injury that has left you dazed or unconscious?

If you're one of those people who say, "Well, I put mine under the deck of my kayak where I can easily get to it in an emergency," I strongly suggest that you find a safe location with no current or under water obstructions, and under the supervision of a competent and experienced kayak instructor/spotter, you flip your kayak and then try putting on your PFD while treading water. --that is, if your kayak hasn't been pushed too far away from you to get to it. Sometimes the flipping kayak and the exiting paddler push the kayak away from the paddler. Putting on a PFD while treading water is not easy! For many people, it would be impossible.

Keep in mind that a PFD is not intended for the expected; it's for those unexpected emergencies when it won't matter if you're a great swimmer. The decision to wear or not wear a PFD affects everyone present, and not just the paddler. If a paddler chooses to forgo wearing a PFD and they later find themselves in an unexpected situation that they did not anticipate and cannot safely handle without a PFD, they have put themselves, and those that attempt to save them, in greater danger.

PINE ACRES LAKE: GOODWIN STATE FOREST

HAMPTON, CT

Paddlers who haven't met their challenge quota for the week, may want to give Pine Acres Lake a go; however, if they're not the type to enjoy a challenge, I suggest passing on this opportunity. The lake is loaded with obstacles, including weeds, stumps, logs, branches, and rocks; however, it is a great bass fishing location. --but you knew that when you saw the list of obstacles, didn't you?

There is a lot of open sun without much shade while paddling on this lake. Early morning or late evening is a good time for bird and wildlife watching; however, the park opens at sunrise and closes at sunset so the prime time for viewing wildlife and birds is limited to areas that can be quickly and easily paddled.

There are also paths, long hiking trails, and places to sit and relax and enjoy nature at this facility.

TYPE: Pond, Bass Fishing

LAUNCH INFO:

The launch is located within the James L. Goodwin State Forest on Potter Road in Hampton, CT The boat ramp and surrounding area is well kept. The road and ramp are tar and there is ample parking and room for trailers to unload and turn around.

LAST PADDLED:

I visited this location on 7/7/14 with my dog; but, had second thoughts about bringing my elderly dog out on the water with so many obstacles to avoid. Needless to say, Tiny was disappointed and did not understand why the kayak was not being unloaded; but quickly perked up when we started down the trail. I have not paddled at this location for several years.

OUR EXPERIENCES:

On my most recent trip to this location, I walked on paths along the pond and surrounding area with my dog. I have paddled here in the past with friends who were fishing. It was very hot in the open sun paddling around in the weeds and other obstacles mentioned above.

NOTES:

POQUETANUCK COVE PRESERVE

LEDYARD/PRESTON, CT

Poquetanuck Cove Preserve provides paddlers with access to the Thames River and the cove itself is a bird watchers paradise! Paddlers are likely to see bald eagles, snowy egrets, ospreys, cormorants, heron, geese, ducks, king fishers, seagulls, swans and more.

This is a tidal area with access to the Thames River so low tide will limit paddlers' access to some northern parts of the cove.

TYPE: Tidal Cove, Nature Preserve, Birding
Thames River Take-out/Put-in

LAUNCH INFO:

There are two launches at this cove:

Northern Launch: From Route 2A, take Cider Mill Road (Avery Hill), then right onto Arrowhead Drive in Ledyard, CT. Go to the end and turn right; paddlers will quickly see the launch and parking area just ahead.

This launch is best used at high tide; use the southern launch at low tide to avoid the silt, sand, and mud that paddlers may have to walk in at the northern launch at low tide.

Southern Launch:
The southern boat launch is located on Route 12 a short distance from where the road crosses the cove in Preston/Gales Ferry, CT. This launch is accessible at high and low tide, but paddlers will have to haul their kayaks farther than they would at high tide. Even at high tide, kayaks need to be carried up a sloping incline to the parking area because boulders prevent paddlers from driving to the water to drop off/take out. The path to the parking area is up a slight incline from the launch area and a bit of a walk compared to the northern launch which allows paddlers to back right up to the water at high tide!

I've used the southern launch as access to the Thames River, paddled round trip from/to the northern launch, and paddled from the northern launch to the southern launch. When paddling the cove, I recommend putting in at one launch and taking out at the opposite launch because this will give paddlers more time to explore; which launch to launch from would be dependent upon the tide. Leaving and returning to the same launch didn't give us enough time to explore all the little inlets and waterways at this location before being restricted by the tide.

This southern launch is a good take-out for a paddle down river from Howard Brown Memorial Park in Norwich, CT *(See page 101 and our experiences for more details)*. This launch can also be used as a put-in to paddle down river to places like the Gold Star Bridge launch *(Page 204)*. There is considerably more boat traffic to contend with down river from Poquetanuck Cove.

LAST PADDLED: 2015 (4x)

OUR EXPERIENCES:

Most recently, we took advantage of an usually warm winter day, and used Poquetanuck Cove as a take-out for a down river paddle from Howard Brown Memorial Park in Norwich. This down river paddle took 4 ½ hours and very easily could have been 5 ½ hours if we had more daylight ahead of us. Conversely, this paddle could be done in less time if paddlers are just paddling through and not taking a break for lunch, investigating things like small coves beyond the railroad tracks, and watching birds and wildlife! The highlight of this January paddle was watching a migrating Harbor Seal watching us from within the choppy water near us. It was a truly amazing experience.

I have done some ice slushing on Poquetanuck Cove in the snowy month of March and I have also paddled it during the warmer summer months. I still can't decide which I enjoyed more, the Bald Eagle flying low overhead or the swan flying up the waterway beside us; both were magnificent! I chuckle whenever I see one of these large swans water walking to take off, and I am always impressed to see them finally airborne after all that effort! We have never paddled at this cove for more than a few minutes without seeing an interesting bird!

The area where we saw the bald eagle and most of the osprey and heron was in the area between the northern and southern boat launches. The other area of interest was beyond the bridge to the right of the northern boat launch where we watched several snowy egrets feeding. We sat and watched them lounge about and feed at a reasonably close distance. This area should be paddled at high tide because access beyond that bridge is restricted during low tide.

We saw ducks, geese, swans, and sea gulls in the area between the northern boat launch and that bridge. We also saw a couple of osprey in this location, but we saw a lot more between the two launches. We paddled under and beyond the other bridge onto Dickermans Brook and in between the tall grasses in the area to the left of it; but, we didn't see much of interest there.

I have experienced wind and tide combining to form choppy water on this cove during our March paddle last season. However, this is not usually the case on calm, sunny days with no wind. On our most recent paddle to this location from the Norwich Marina, the Thames River was quite choppy; however, we entered the cove and it was calm.

Just outside this cove, to the right on the Thames River behind tiny Walden Island, can be seen the remains of one of two ships on this river. The remains of the other ship are located closer to the Howard Brown Memorial Park launch up river *(Photo page 217)*.

NOTES:

QUADDICK LAKE: THE BACK DOOR IN!

THOMPSON, CT

Quaddick Lake has a main entrance; however, this back entrance to the lake is handy during those times in which the main entrance is packed with lake goers! Most recently, we used this access to paddle on Stump Pond and then on Quaddick Lake on the busy 4th of July weekend! Main entrance also listed below.

TYPE: Lake, Bass Fishing

LAUNCH INFO:

The back door launch to Quaddick Lake: Take Brandy Hill Road off Route 193 in Thompson, CT. Stay left at the Thompson Rod and Gun Club and follow Baker Road to the bridge. Baker Road will turn into a dirt road, and shortly after, paddlers will see the launch on the left just before the bridge.

The launch is located within the pond referred to as "Stump Pond" which is part of the upper section of the Quaddick Lake waterway. Utilizing the launch on Stump Pond, paddlers can then paddle under the bridge near the launch to enter "Middle Pond" which is part of Quaddick Lake or paddle left to paddle Stump Pond.

The Quaddick Lake main boat launch is located within Quaddick State Park, which is located on Quaddick Town Farm Road in Thompson, CT.

LAST PADDLED: 7/5/15

OUR EXPERIENCE:

Being the July 4th holiday weekend, we expected the main entrance and boat launch area of Quaddick State Park to be overwhelmingly busy; so, we entered Quaddick Lake from the launch on Stump Pond. We paddled around Stump Pond and to the back of Thompson Speedway before returning to the bridge and paddling on Quaddick Lake.

Stump Pond is of a paddleable size. I enjoyed paddling around it and investigating some waterways off this pond; however, I was disappointed to find barrels, old racing tires, and other debris in the water near the speedway. I was literally jerked to a stop when I unknowingly rammed a full barrel just beneath the water's surface. We located 2 other barrels and some racing tires floating partially submerged in that same area.

There are some interesting waterways among the weeds in that back section where we did some bird watching. A late fall paddle to Stump Pond will demonstrate why it is named as it is; other times of the year, paddlers will only see a few stumps here and there.

The main body of Quaddick Pond is moderately populated and was very active with boat traffic as we expected would be the case on a holiday weekend. I saw two different fisherman catch large mouth bass while on Quaddick Lake. One fishermen by the bridge told me that he has also caught Calico Bass there. They recommended using shiners.

QUIAMBAUG COVE

STONINGTON, CT

Quiambaug Cove's shoreline is sparsely to moderately occupied with homes, stretches of woodland and swamp, and the Knox Preserve/Avalonia Land Conservancy. I cannot vouch for boat activity or the overall conditions usually found at this cove because this was my first paddle at this location. Our experience here was very peaceful and relaxing; however, this might have been due to the time of year and forthcoming forecast of heavy rain.

Beyond the railroad bridge is coastal access to open water and not a place for new or inexperienced paddlers! Only well seasoned paddlers with appropriate equipment and gear should be exploring beyond the railroad bridge at Quiambaug Cove.

TYPE: Tidal Cove, Coastal Access , Adjoining Nature Preserve

LAUNCH INFO:

The boat launch is located at the separation in the sequence of guard rails across the road from the Quiambaug Professional Center on Wilcox Road in Stonington, CT. The launch is a gravel incline from the road to the water with a level area of pea gravel like material beneath the water. This level area beneath the water was perfect for entering and exiting my floating kayak. We unloaded and parked across the way in the QPC parking lot which only had 2 other vehicles in it to avoid parking on the trimmed grass roadside.

LAST PADDLED: 12/17/15

OUR EXPERIENCES:

It took about 3 hours to casually paddle about the upper and lower cove and investigate inlet pathways.

We don't usually expect to encounter many boaters out on the water in December; however, we didn't even see one person, on shore nor boating, during our entire paddle. We did see numerous geese and a few ducks hanging out with the larger birds. There is an osprey nesting station near the southern end of the cove; however we did not see any osprey during this winter paddle.

We experienced the start of high tide while paddling the cove. The onset of high tide didn't seem to affect the conditions within the cove as much as other coves we've paddled because the water coming into the cove must come in under the small railroad bridge opening; so, the water within the cove didn't get choppy except in the immediate area of the bridge. I caution less experienced paddlers to realize that the current being forced under that bridge can be strong and significant during the onset of tidal change and certain weather conditions.

We did not explore the other side of the railroad bridge because when we arrived at the bridge heavy fog was rolling in and heavy rain was due in the area within the hour; these conditions combined with the onset of high tide could be a recipe for mishap so we turned back! We might paddle beyond the railroad bridge when we return in the summer to check out the adjacent Knox Preserve.

QUINEBAUG POND
(WAUREGAN RESERVOIR)

DANIELSON, CT

Paddle to the middle of this oval pond, spin, and paddlers will have seen most of what there is to be seen here. There is a day camp at the far right end and a railroad track that runs along one shore, lots of trees, two swimming areas, and the boat ramp. Paddling at this location is primarily for fishing. I sometimes paddle at this location with people and dogs who are new to kayaking.

TYPE: Pond, Fishing, Swimming

LAUNCH INFO:

The launch is located within the Quinebaug Pond State Park on Shepard Hill Road in Danielson, CT. It has an accessible boat launch that can accommodate trailer unloading and offers an easy launching experience. **NOTE:** I've seen vehicles ticketed by the warden for having been parked too close to the ramp on more than one occasion! Heed the signs!

The entrance sign and maps will state Quinebaug Pond; however, the locals sometimes refer to it as the Wauregan Reservoir--so if you get lost, and the person to which you're asking directions looks at you like you have two heads, ask for directions to the Wauregan Reservoir.

LAST PADDLED: Spring 2014

OUR EXPERIENCES:

This reservoir is a kayaking experience that I would only recommend for people who are fishing or those who are fairly new to kayaking. I last paddled here in 2014 with my dog and a person who was new to kayaking.

I would not recommend this location for experienced paddlers who are looking for something of real substance and interest. Paddlers might occasionally see something of interest: however, it pretty much looks the same all the way around it. I've been swimming at this location far more often than I've paddled this pond.

NOTES:

QUINEBAUG RIVER
CONNECTICUT BOAT LAUNCHES

Novice river paddlers: There are a few Quinebaug River sites that could be appropriate for some experienced flat water paddlers who are new to river paddling. These sites are: Riverside Park, Butts Bridge, Aspinook Pond, and Canterbury Bridge to Butts Bridge. _Read all cautions first!_ Novice paddlers should paddle with an experienced river paddler who has experience paddling these sections of the Quinebaug River and also wear a PFD and emergency whistle. Rivers can sometimes appear to be mundane to inexperienced river paddlers, when in reality, the situation can be potentially dangerous.

Thompson, CT: Fabyan Dam

This put-in is on the opposite side of the bridge from the dam on Fabyan Road in Fabyan (Thompson), CT. There is a small paved parking area adjacent to the moderately sloping ramp to the water.

Caution: Swift current and class 1 rapids. Paddling from this launch is generally a spring paddle because water levels may not be high enough later in the season. However, very high water levels after a spring thaw can make this paddle significantly more challenging!

The take-out for this trip is the West Thompson Lake boat launch.

The portage area is river left approaching the dam. Please scout this portage before attempting to use it because it is near an open spillway in the dam and the resulting current can be fast at times. Put-in for this portage is located near the bridge on West Dudley Road in Dudley MA. This section includes fast water and Class 1 rapids. Scout river--water can be too low later in the paddling season. Not for beginners.

West Thompson Lake, Thompson, CT: Dam/Lake

This is the take-out for the Fabyan Launch and also for paddling around West Thompson Lake (*See page 207*). Paddlers can also paddle up river from this launch/lake for as far as current and water level will allow.

The West Thompson Lake launch is located on Campground Drive off Reardon Road in Thompson, CT. Follow signs from Reardon Road. There is a large sand/gravel parking area and launch with ample parking for car top and trailers. Seasonal camping www.recreation.gov and chemical toilets are available at this location.

Caution: It is not advisable to attempt to paddle down river from this location due to hazardous conditions and two significant dams/falls!

Putnam, CT: Simonzi Park

This is a **put-in** for a down river trip from this location. The launch is located at Simonzi Park on Kennedy Drive in Putnam, CT. Seasonal chemical toilets and optional steps down a moderate slope to the water.

This section of river is best paddled early in the paddling season because later in the summer, there can be sections where the water can be too low and paddlers could scrape the bottoms of their kayaks on rocks and/or end up pulling their kayaks along behind them. Rock dodging becomes more of an issue with lower water levels. At very low water levels, the exposed rocks can make it impossible to paddle some sections safely. Conversely, very high water levels immediately following a spring thaw could create unexpected or dangerous conditions as well.

There are two Pomfret, CT options for **take outs** (*See below*).

Pomfret, CT: Two take-outs:

The take-out at Cotton Bridge has less parking than the Route 101 take-out which is about a mile down river; however, the Route 101 take out can be a tricky with high water levels and faster current.

The informal launch/take out at Cotton Bridge is located river right after passing under Cotton Bridge which is located on Cotton Bridge Road in Pomfret Center, CT. I prefer this launch over the formal Route 101 launch a mile down river *(See below)*. It's only short-fall is parking. Paddlers can also paddle up river for as long as current allows.

The Route 101 formal launch/take-out is located about a mile down river from Cotton Bridge and is river right after passing under the Route 101 bridge near Litchfield Avenue in Pomfret, CT. This formal launch has a set of steps leading directly to the water. The last step is a dilly! I personally do not recommend launching or exiting a kayak there, especially during strong current. Facing the water at this launch, paddlers will see a path to the right of those steps; a short distance down that path is where many paddlers choose to exit and enter. Paddlers who use the spot at the end of that path may get their feet wet; but, it's usually easier than dealing with that last step at the formal launch area. Paddlers can paddle up river for as long as current allows.

Caution: The section of river between Route 101 and Brooklyn should not be paddled until which time a formal portage is created at the Rogers Dam. There is no "formal" portage at the Rogers Dam and it has a significant and dangerous drop! It can be portaged river right; however, it requires paddlers use a dangerously steep and very narrow path. The current leading up to the dam can be strong and significant at times, making this a potentially dangerous place to attempt to portage as well. During some times of the year, the water level below the dam can be too shallow to easily paddle as well. During times when the water level is higher, the area immediately after the dam can be swift and rough *(See Riverside Park below)*.

Brooklyn, CT: Riverside Park:

Caution: The Danielson Falls are a very short distance down river from this launch near the Route 6 bridge. Stay back from the bridge and dam/falls which is **EXTREMELY DANGEROUS!**

The Brooklyn boat ramp for this section of the Quinebaug River is located on Greenway Drive in Brooklyn, CT. I have paddled here several times and the launch is always well maintained and is part of a very small park with ample parking. The ramp is gravel with a cement slab at the point of entry.

This launch <u>does not</u> currently provide paddlers with access to other launches; perhaps at some point, when/if a formal portage is created at the Rogers Dam, this can become a take-out for the Putnam and Route 101 launches. Until that time, it is a singular launch.

I have paddled up river from this location a few times; however, I have never made it to the Rogers falls without bottoming out due to low water or meeting a current I couldn't paddle against. I've gotten close; but, I've never made it to the falls. Late spring is probably the best time to attempt paddling up river when the water level is still high due to the spring thaw; although, the current may then hinder progress as well.

Paddlers who are unfamiliar with this area of the river, and wish to give this up river paddle a go, could use a GPS APP to locate the main entry to the river. There are a few different water ways beyond the initial two islands that can mislead paddlers into dead end inlets off the main river; after that, the route is more obvious.

Killingly, CT: Little League Field

Put in for a down river paddle to Plainfield Fish Hatchery, Canterbury Bridge, Butts Bridge, or Aspinook Pond. **Read all cautions below!**

Hazards!

Not a place for beginners! This section of river has a variety of conditions that can be challenging, and in some cases, potentially hazardous to paddlers. Paddlers must, under some conditions, avoid dangerous remnants of old dams as well as maneuvering class I and II rapids, faster current, and rock dodging. Lower water levels can bring the remaining pieces of the old dams closer to the surface where they are more likely to be an issue.

Flipping at the site of one of these former dams could mean being injured by pieces of the old dams sticking up from the bottom of the river. During low water levels, I have seen what looks like rebar at one site and there can be large pieces of stone and concrete at these sites, as well as, down river from these locations.

What remains of the former Dyer Dam is located in the river behind the current Phaiah Dog Park in Killingly, CT. Remnants of this dam can be clearly seen river right and left as well as rapids the width of the river. Very soon after this former dam will be the remnants of another dam which may not even be noticeable at high water levels; but, may require some serious rock dodging or portaging in some low water conditions. The Wauregan Dam was located a short distance up river from the Route 205 bridge in Wauregan, CT. River left, paddlers will see large stone and cement structures related to the old dam and mill, and will experience strong current and rapids in this same area.

Scouting this section of river:

Paddlers should thoroughly scout this section, checking water level, current, rapids, exposed rocks, and possible conditions related to the remains of the former dams prior to attempting to paddle this section of river. I suggest checking conditions up river from the bridge on Route 205 in Wauregan first because the current and rapids are most severe at the former site of that mill dam.

Paddlers can park in the small hard surface pull off area on the down river side of the Route 205 bridge, walk down the washed out path to the base of the bridge, and walk under to the other side *(if this section is too wet, the next section/passage under this bridge is sandy and usually dry)*. From there, paddlers can make their way along the raised path *(right)* or along the wooded shoreline of the river to the site of the former mill and dam, and have a closer look at the situation.

If after reviewing this area, experienced river paddlers think that this might be too much for them, they should not consider paddling this section; however, if experienced river paddlers think this section looks suitable for their skill set and physical condition, they can walk the Quinebaug River Trail and check out the northern section of this part of the river. The Quinebaug River Trail can be accessed at Phaiah Dog Park on Quinebaug Lane off Route 12 in Danielson, CT and at the put-in launch for this paddle *(See below)*.

It's important to scout the river shortly before paddling it because high or low water will change conditions. For example, during a summer visit to the dog park, my dog loved playing and rolling in the shallow river conditions found in the river left of the fenced dog areas; however, it would not have been a great time to paddle this section of the river because it was only a little more than ankle deep! Low water conditions will also bring the remains of the old dams closer to the surface of the water, and potentially be more dangerous to paddlers.

The next launch is in Plainfield *(below)* and conditions at that location can also give paddlers some indications regarding water level, current, and other conditions by walking along the river at that location.

Launch: The Killingly/Danielson boat ramp for the Quinebaug River is located on the Quinebaug River Trail behind the sewage treatment plant and Little League field on Rte 12 in Danielson, CT. If the gate is open, vehicles can be driven behind the concession stand to the point where the sign states no vehicles beyond this point, unloaded, and then parked in the parking lot. The launch is to the left and off the far side of the walking/bike path and has a slight slope with a nice gravel point of entry.

Plainfield, CT: Plainfield Fish Hatchery

The section of river between this location and Robert Manship Park is a beautiful stretch of river; however, it does involve some white water and rock dodging. Paddlers will likely see birds and wildlife; however, it is not a great birding location due to the faster current.

The Plainfield boat launch for the Quinebaug River can be found by driving past the Plainfield Fish Hatchery located on Trout Hatchery Road in Central Village, CT; go RIGHT after the first Pasture Pond sign, continuing on until points of entry to the river can be seen on the right; the first area has a sign designating it as being part of the "Quinebaug Valley Canoe Trail.

At some times of the year, this water is very shallow and it might make entry a bit tricky or even impossible. I have walked in the water to get to/from deep enough water to launch from this location; however, that is an indicator of low levels to come further along this paddling route.

Later in the season, the rock dodging becomes even more of an issue and sometimes paddlers may find the water is too low to make this trek. I suggest checking the water level north of the take out at Robert Manship Park before paddling this section of river. If when looking up river from that bridge, paddlers see a lot of exposed rock and shallow water, I suggest putting this paddle off until the following spring.

Paddlers can paddle from this location to the Robert Manship Park in Canterbury or continue on to further destinations, such as, Butts Bridge and Aspinook Pond. Current dictates how fast this can be paddled; Plainfield to Canterbury usually takes between 2 ½ hours.

Canterbury,CT: Robert Manship Park (Canterbury Bridge)

The Quinebaug River boat launch area at Canterbury Bridge is located on Rte 14 near the Canterbury/Plainfield town line at the Robert Manship Park. *See page 175 for a more detailed description.*

This is a possible take-out for a paddle from an upriver locations such as the Plainfileld Fish Hatchery and the Killingly Launch *(See potential HAZARDS for Killingly launch above)*. It is also a possible put-in to paddle down river to Butts Bridge or Aspinook Pond. Paddling from this location to Butts Bridge takes about 3 hours; However, time is strongly dependant upon current; it could be paddled faster than that if paddlers are utilizing the spring current and just paddling straight through without taking time to check out the beautiful surroundings, wildlife watching, and shooting photos. Aspinook Pond is about ½ hour paddle down river from the Butts Bridge launch; the Aspinook launch cannot be seen from the river because it is located within a sheltered cove river left. *(See page 21)*

Canterbury, CT: Butts Bridge

The Butts Bridge Quinebaug River boat launch area is located on Butts Bridge Road, Canterbury, CT. The dirt entry road near the large green bridge is bumpy with several pot holes so drive slow. There is ample parking and room for trailers. The launch area is basically an extension of the gravel parking area which extends down and into the water.

This is generally a take-out point from the Killingly, Plainfield, or Canterbury Launches; however, later in the season it is possible to paddle up river from this location. This launch is about a ½ hour paddle from Aspinook Pond *(below)* I have paddled to/from this location countless times. *(See Butts Bridge feature entry Page 51).*

Griswold, CT: Aspinook Pond

The Griswold boat ramp for the Quinebaug River is located on Arbor Road in Griswold CT. From Rte 12 in Griswold, take Quinebaug Camp Road, then left onto Arbor Road. The launch area is located almost at the end of Arbor Road. Carefully watch for the narrow dirt/gravel launch road on the right. This is basically a dirt/gravel road which ends at the water. This launch is not visible from the river because it is located within a sheltered cove. *(See page 21 for more details.)*

Jewett City, CT: Slater Mill

Please read all of this entry in its entirety! There could be life threatening hazards to those paddlers who may attempt to paddle

this section. **It should NOT be paddled under current conditions.**
Paddlers who are considering a paddle on this stretch of river should
NOT use the information that I provided as their only source of
information and they should do extensive scouting of the entire section
first. I have scouted this section of the Quinebaug River; however, I
have never paddled it.

The potential unofficial put-in below the Aspinook Dam is located within
the dirt parking area behind Slater Mill in Jewett City, CT, and is only a
short drive from the Aspinook launch. The mill currently consists of
stores and a Flea Market. Enter and proceed to the dirt parking area in
back of the mill, turn left and proceed to its farthest point. The potential
informal launch area is located down a path to the river along that far
end. It is rustic, a bit of a walk, and primarily used as a local fishing
spot. Paddlers may have to search for it because summer foliage can
easily block if from view. Kids in the area will know where it is.

Theoretically, the take-out for this trip would be the Greenville Dam
portage/launch area on the Shetucket River or the Howard Brown
Memorial Park located on the Thames River in Norwich, CT. However,
I know of at least a few potentially hazardous obstacles for a down river
paddle on this section of the Quinebaug River.

Hazard 1: Some areas of this trip do not supply a paddler with a choice
about quitting once they have committed to this paddle because there
are often high river banks and current moving the paddler along as well
as rock dodging at certain water levels. I've seen ankle deep water for
as far as I could see at the initial launch site in Jewett City and at other
spots along this potential paddling route. However, higher water in the
spring means stronger current and rapids and rock dodging.

Hazard 2: There is a significant Dam/falls located just before the point
where the Quinebaug River converges with the Shetucket River and
there is currently no formal portage at that location. It is preceded by
high river banks and is bordered on one side by a railroad track and the
plant which operates the dam on the other side.

I have paddled up the Shetucket River and into the mouth of the Quinebaug River where it converges with the Shetucket River to get a different perspective of this situation; however, the water level in that area was extremely low with uneven large slippery rocks to contend with. It looked to me that getting back into the water after any type of portage would mean maneuvering kayaks down very steep inclines to the water, and most likely by way of the active railroad track.

If someone were to make it past the falls/dam and maneuver down the steep embankments, slippery large and uneven rocks with water too low to paddle or high strong current could be the next potential hazard to be dealt with. This dam and the other functioning dams on the Shetucket River can all affect what goes on at this re-entry point!

Hazard 3: These issues may not be the entirety of what exists within that stretch of river. There may be unknown hazards as well There are functioning dams involved which also add an unpredictable variable that could create unknown hazards. Successfully paddling this section of river would require timing and a perfect set of circumstances involving several unpredictable variables. Under the current conditions, I see this paddle as a bad gamble and one that should not be undertaken.

It is important to thoroughly scout the area reasonably close to any attempt to paddle it because seasonal changes greatly affect certain parts of this section of river; if scouted during one time of the year and attempted to paddle in another, paddlers could be facing very different challenges! Scouting during both high and low water levels would allow potential paddlers the opportunity to see what is under the high water. This is definitely not a place for beginners, and I have my doubts about the safety of anyone who may decide to try it under the current conditions. I strongly suggest avoiding this section of river.

Remember, just because someone may say they paddled a section of river, doesn't mean it was a smart or safe thing to do! Be safe!

Greenville Dam: (Page 85) Howard Brown Launch (Page 101)

Quonnie Beach

QUONOCHONTAUG
(QUONNIE SALT POND)

TO

QUONNIE BEACH

CHARLESTOWN, RI

Yes, Quonochontaug, or "Quonnie" Pond, and Quonnie Beach are located in Rhode Island; but just barely, and such a fun paddle that I must include it!

Paddlers who hang around with me long enough, will eventually hear me say that they can't always judge a paddle by the view from the launch! Quonnie Salt Pond is such a place! Quonnie Salt Pond offers paddlers easy access to the coastal Quonnie Beach...and paddlers won't see that access from the launch! *(See photo previous page)*.

It is the quick and easy access to the coastal Quonnie Beach that makes this a great paddling destination! The launch at this salt pond is adjacent to the breach and access to Quonnie Beach is on the opposite side of that breach; however, do not attempt to paddle straight across the breach opening to get to it because there is a sandy shallow area that runs along that shoreline from the far side of the breach opening well into the pond. It could be extremely dangerous to maneuver from the breach to/from that shallow area, especially if paddlers were to fall into the breach.

Please take a few extra minutes to paddle to the right of the launch and go around that shallow sandy area adjacent to the breach. It will be necessary to cross that sandy shallow area; but, cross it from the pond and not the breach area! Paddlers can see hints of this shallow sandy area and sometimes see birds resting on higher portions of it.

Entry to the coastal beach will be found along the shallow shoreline on the opposite side of the breach from the launch. Paddlers should look for a beachy looking area among a grassy stretch of shoreline. Up over the hill is Quonnie Beach! The only access to this beach is by boat, foot, or 4 wheel drive along the beach!

TYPE: Salt Pond, Coastal access to Quonnie Beach!

LAUNCH INFO:

The launch for Quonochontaug Pond, also known as Quonnie Salt Pond, is located at the end of West Beach Road (turns to dirt) off Route 1 in Charlestown, RI.

Cautions: The Quonnie Pond Launch is at the entrance to the breach. Paddlers without experience paddling in a breach, should stay away from it! The purpose of a breach is to allow open water access for large boats. The conditions within the breach can change in minutes due to large boats passing through, the tide, weather, etc. When the start of high or low tide really kicks in, it can be like a bath tub draining or filling; but, on a much larger scale. Add wind, large boats, and other unforeseen conditions, and paddling in the breach can be a potentially dangerous situation. Paddle right from the launch and stay away from the breach!

LAST PADDLED: 10/12/15

OUR EXPERIENCES:

There were only 3 other paddlers visiting Quonnie beach when we last visited this site on an unseasonably warm October day *(Photo page 169)*. Having the beach to ourselves was amazing.

I've paddled around Quonnie Salt Pond once and ½ way around on another occasion, and for the most part, that aspect of it is quite usual and expected. However, I was surprised to see an amazing number of cormorants at this location!

On one occasion the tide and wind combined to created choppy conditions that sloshed water up and over my kayak as I paddled around the salt pond; so, under certain conditions, a kayak skirt might be appropriate.

It is the passage to Quonnie Beach that makes this paddle special!

PADDLERS SAFETY TIP

Every adult paddler should bring a knife with them! It could, at some point, save the carrier of that knife or a paddling friend.

I have a single edged kitchen knife sheathed inside a section of pool noodle which is firmly squeezed under my kayak seat. I can remove this knife, slice a tow rope, dog leash, paddle leash, another paddlers rope or cord, in seconds, if an emergency involving a rope or cord were to arise.

Envision if you can, towing a supply pod or kayak loaded with supplies behind a kayak. The supply kayak or pod, for whatever reason, starts sinking, putting the paddler and their kayak in jeopardy. The knot or clip that connects it to their kayak is now pulled too tight to unclip or untie it--what do they do? Well, if they have a knife and they can reach the tow rope, they can cut the line before it puts the paddler and their kayak in further danger. They are then in a position where they can more safely address the situation.

Note: I run tow ropes through a tow ring at the end of my kayak and secure the tow line close behind me where I can reach it in case it needs to be cut. This extra length of floating cut line can also make it easier to regain control of the previously towed item as well.

RED CEDAR LAKE
MOOWEEN STATE PARK

LEBANON, CT

Red Cedar lake adjoins Mooween State Park in Lebanon, CT. It is primarily a bass fishing spot. From a recreational paddling perspective, it doesn't have as much to offer as nearby Williams Lake also located in Lebanon *(See page 211)*. However, the hiking trails at Mooween State Park are interesting for those paddlers who have an imagination, love history, and like to walk in the woods.

Mooween State Park was once a boy scout camp, and some remains of that camp, such as steps to no where, ball courts, pieces of foundation, and an old chimney (said to be from before the camp was built), can be seen while hiking the wooded trails. Also be aware that the park offers hunting; so, use caution in that area during hunting season.

Red Cedar Lake is very quiet and peaceful, yet it's not quite big enough to fully absorb that feeling before seeing the entire lake. The colorful fall foliage surrounding the lake offers a spectacular backdrop to a fall paddle at this location; however, paddlers can literally sit in the middle of this lake, spin in a circle and see most of it. One side is wooded and the other side moderately populated and there are a couple of small inlet areas towards the back left of the pond.

TYPE: Pond, Fishing

LAUNCH INFO:

The boat launch is located at the entrance to Mooween State Park on Camp Mooween Road in Lebanon, CT. The 2 launch areas between the boulders at this location initially look narrow, however, I had no problem getting my kayak through and I watched a fisherman launch a flat bottom boat using the one on the right facing the pond.

LAST PADDLED: 9/29/14

OUR EXPERIENCES:

My dog, Tiny, enjoyed a couple of the inlet areas from the deck of my kayak where we saw ducks and turtles, a small island, and stumps both above and below the water. One inlet was thick with lily pads, and we ventured through it in the hopes of seeing some wildlife; however, we only saw the same ducks that we had startled earlier on the open lake.

This might be the go-to-spot for paddlers who are interested in combining a paddling session with walking trails and fishing! Paddlers who are looking to paddle and not also fish or walk the trails, might find nearby Williams Lake to be of more interest *(See page 211)*.

NOTES:

ROBERT MANSHIP PARK:
QUINEBAUG RIVER

CANTERBURY, CT

Some of the local Quinebaug River boat launches, such as Aspinook Pond, Butts Bridge and Riverside Park, can be paddled from, and back to, the same launch during certain times of the year; however, that is not the case with this launch. The current is too swift to paddle up river from this location and it is often very shallow as well, especially later in the season when water levels recede.

The current that paddlers immediately experience heading down river from this launch is generally the fastest current to be experienced during the entire down river paddle from this location. This faster moving section ends after only a few curves in the river below this launch. Potential paddlers can best view this current a short distance from the Plainfield side of the bridge where the river loops back towards the road. There is a fishing pull off area along that stretch of road and a path along the river which can provide an even closer look.

Paddlers shouldn't let the idea of an easy spring current fool them into thinking that they won't have to paddle when going down river from this launch. LOL! Unless there has been significant snow fall over the winter, the current in this portion of the Quinebaug is not usually consistently moving paddlers right along. There will be areas where it will, and then long stretches where paddlers will have to paddle. Even in the areas where it is moving, paddlers will likely feel the need to lightly paddle to move along faster.

This is a beautiful meandering section of river that affords paddlers opportunities to see lots of birds and wildlife, such as osprey, eagles, hawks, heron, ducks, deer, muskrats, and even beaver. There are a few houses, an apartment building, and fields within this section; however, they are typically blocked from the paddler's view by summer foliage. In the spring, paddlers may see things like an old chimney *(river left)* and the buildings and fields mentioned above.

In the late summer and fall months of the year, the current found beyond the initial burst of current at the Robert Manship Launch, is usually almost non-existent. In fact, I have paddled with my dog from Butts Bridge up river to that swifter moving area just prior to the Robert Manship Launch and back to Butts Bridge later in the paddling season. The reduced current in this area is due to the looping fashion in which this river flows through the landscape. The water level decreases as the season progresses and, as a result, rocks will be closer to the surface; canoes may even bottom out later in the paddling season if there hasn't been a lot of rain.

The Aspinook Pond take-out is about ½ hour paddle beyond the Butts Bridge take-out, and the entire trip from Robert Manship Park to Aspinook Pond takes about 3 - 3 ½ hours with an easy spring current. Of course, this time depends upon how much lingering and paddling is done! I have never paddled straight through without lingering, exploring, and watching birds and wildlife.

TYPE: Quinebaug River Boat Launch *(down river access only),* Bird & Wildlife watching, Fishing

LAUNCH INFO:

Put in:

Robert Manship Park at Canterbury Bridge, is located on Route 14 at the Canterbury/Plainfield town line near the Rte 169 intersection with Route 14.

Take out 1:

The Butts Bridge boat launch is located between the start and end point of this trip and is located at the end of a dirt road by the large green metal bridge on Butts Bridge Road in Canterbury, CT *(See page 51).*

I prefer the Butts Bridge take-out over the Aspinook Pond launch. Shortly after Butts Bridge, the shoreline becomes more and more populated and less visually interesting and large motor boats along with jet skiers tend to utilize Aspinook Pond and the area below Butts Bridge. Some jet skiers and large motor boats will occasionally be seen in the area of Butts Bridge; however, the larger motor boats can't safely maneuver around the shallower conditions and under water obstacles above Butts Bridge.

Take out 2:

The end point is Aspinook Pond *(See page 21)* which is located on Arbor Road in Griswold CT. From Rte 12, take Quinebaug Camp Road then left onto Arbor Road. The entrance to the launch area is a small dirt road on the right almost at the end of Arbor Road. About half way down the dirt entry, paddlers will see a sign that reads, "Closed at sunset...," and the launch will be just ahead.

Parking is limited to a few vehicles. Not a great place for a trailer; but, one could fit if the paddler can easily back a trailer and other parked vehicles are not in the way. The entry point is very visible when there are no leaves on the trees; but, easily missed among summer foliage.

From the river: The Aspinook launch is located within a small cove river left; for this reason the launch is not visible from the river. Unless paddlers are very familiar with the location of this sheltered cove, they should use a GPS to locate it as they paddle down river or mark the cove entrance before starting the trip. In the spring, paddlers may see, and more easily identify, the entrance to this cove; however, the inlet for this cove is more likely to be over looked among summer foliage due to the island in the middle of it. I've done it, and I know where it is!

LAST PADDLED: 2/29/16

OUR EXPERIENCES:

I have never taken anyone on this spring paddle who hasn't enjoyed it, including my dog! In fact, Tiny has spent many hours on this river with me. Most recently, a friend and I got caught in the rain at a more northern launch; so, we quickly drove down to this more southern launch which was also at the tail end of the storm clouds. We paddled to Butts Bridge and were rewarded with a few sprinkles, separating clouds and bright sunshine, as well as, muskrat, swan, and heron sightings.

I've done frivolous things like float down this section of river reading a book or with my feet up on deck and my dog sprawled out between them and my metal detector trailing along beside us. I've even paddled this section of river beneath a full moon.

This may seem gross to some; but, during one trip, I watched an eagle feed on a deer carcass that was caught within half a tree and floating down this section of river. The eagle was magnificent and I had never had the opportunity to be so close to a feeding eagle. I was literally only the distance of the width of the river away from it because I came upon it from up river while it was looking down and it didn't hear me; one of the advantages of paddling alone! I've also seen osprey, eagles, hawks, heron, ducks, geese, muskrat, deer, swans and signs of beaver.

On another occasion, later in the season, a friend and I heard a big ruckus going in a little cove; after slowly maneuvering into the cove, we found that the ruckus was being caused by large carp flipping, twisting and turning, and some breaching the water around us. We floated within the cove with this activity going on around us on all sides. They acted as if we weren't even there! This was also something that I had never seen before.

ROGERS LAKE

OLD LYME, CT

Rogers Lake is about 260 acres and located in Old Lyme, CT. This lake is known for bass fishing; however, it is moderately to heavily populated along much of its shoreline except the most northern section near Blood Street. This lake has five small islands on it and the largest island has a summer cottage in the middle of it.

TYPE: Pond, Bass Fishing

LAUNCH INFO:

This DEEP launch is located at 102 Grassy Hill Road in Old Lyme, CT. There is a parking area suitable for car top and trailers and an easy access cement ramp. Paddle left from the launch and into the open lake. Paddle right after entering the open lake and then bear left to enter the less populated area of this lake.

LAST PADDLED: Prior to 2014

OUR EXPERIENCES:

Overall, there is no feeling of getting away from it all here. My only recommendation for this lake would be fishing. From a recreational paddling perspective, I would recommend nearby Lord Cove *(Page 119)*. I have paddled Rogers Lake with friends who were fishing and I have seen people ice fishing on this lake; but, I have never done so myself.

PADDLING SAFETY TIP

When paddlers are using an unfamiliar kayak, they should adjust foot rests and do a safety pre-check, then if it's safe to do so, try out the kayak in a safe area with no current and no obstructions beneath the surface. If it is safe to do so, explore things like the tipping point and turning radius of the kayak and assess how well it is balanced in the water. <u>Beginners should only do this with an experienced spotter</u>. This knowledge could help paddlers paddle more confidently and effectively, and it could be helpful information in an emergency situation.

ROSELAND PARK POND

WOODSTOCK, CT

Roseland Pond is almost 100 acres and a sit-in-spin, lightly populated, and not much to it; however, the park is an inviting little place, including picnic tables, a children's play area, benches along the water's edge, and a fire pit which was lit on the chilly Autumn afternoon in which we last visited. There is a golf course across the street and a kid's ball park connected to the small park.

Most lakes and ponds in Woodstock are not open to the public for boating purposes. To my knowledge Roseland Pond is the only pond, of its size or larger, that doesn't require a Woodstock resident permit sticker on boats used on them. Paddlers who visit Woodstock, CT, should bring their own Dunkin coffee because none of the more traditional fast-food restaurants and convenience stores will be found there.

TYPE: Pond, Park

LAUNCH INFO:

The boat launch is located within Roseland Park on Roseland Park Road in Woodstock, CT. The launch is to the far left when facing the pond and consisted of loose rock and dirt when I last visited this site. At some point, this situation might improve after the rocks eventually settle into the dirt; but at the point in time when I last visited, it was not something to be driven on and there were a few deep ruts from others who had tried. I parked at the top of the slight incline and carried my kayak down the short distance to the water to avoid this situation.

Online, the town's Roseland Cottage web page stated that the park closed as sunset; but, on one occasion when we were visiting the park, the on-site sign stated gate closed at 5:00 pm which was before sunset on that day. It was the type of sign that the time can be changed so this is something to be aware of if paddling on the pond because the boat launch and its parking area are well inside the park gate in question. It would be a long haul to bring a kayak from the outer parking area, to the launch, and back to that parking area outside that gate; but, not impossible.

LAST PADDLED: 11/11/14

OUR EXPERIENCES:

During our last visit, we met several friendly people and my dog, Tiny, was happy to meet a few dogs being walked along the trail connecting the park to the ball park after we paddled the pond. I wouldn't recommend kayaking on this pond unless fishing; but, if paddlers are in the area and feel like spending some time in the outdoors this little park might be the place to go. The park has a charming family atmosphere and the people we encountered openly engaged us in conversation; we were even invited to join the group around the fire.

I have spent hours relaxing and chatting with my paddling friends over tea and scones at nearby Mrs. Bridges Pantry. Mrs. Bridges Pantry is located near the fairgrounds on nearby Route 169 in Woodstock, CT. We occasionally stop there on our way to and from paddling destinations and sometimes make the trip to Woodstock just for this purpose.

NOTES:

ROSS POND:
OLD FURNACE STATE PARK

DANIELSON, CT

The park has two ponds and they are not accessed through the main entrance to the park *(see launch info below)*. The smaller pond is too small for paddling; however, standing by this small pond and looking up at an autumn display of color over Ross Cliffs is stunning.

The larger of the two ponds makes for a beautiful fall paddle; however, most of it can be seen from the center of the pond. There is a bit more to be seen in a little inlet area and also under the tunnel to the back left of the pond. Beyond the tunnel which goes under the nearby highway, paddlers can see beaver huts, ducks, and if they're lucky maybe a beaver.

There are also hiking trails that go up around the top of Ross Cliffs and throughout portions of the park. These hiking trails can be accessed through the main park entrance on South Frontage Road, or they can be accessed on the far side of the smaller pond. Caution should be used when hiking at this location. The cliffs, some inclines, and some crevices can be potentially dangerous. A classmate of mine died falling from Ross Cliffs when I was a kid. There have been other deaths and serious injuries there as well.

TYPE: Pond

LAUNCH INFO:

Ross Pond is located within Old Furnace State Park in Danielson, CT.

However, Ross Pond boat launch is not accessed through the main entrance for Old Furnace State Park. From Rte 6 in Danielson CT, take South Frontage Road, pass the main park entrance on the right; then watch for the boat launch sign and turn right onto Ross Road. Oddly enough, paddlers will not see a boat launch sign when coming from the other direction on South Frontage Road. Parking will be at the end with the launch located to the left and the smaller pond slightly out of sight and to the right below Ross Cliffs.

LAST PADDLED: 10/15/14

OUR EXPERIENCES:

I spent a lot of time here as a kid. Ross Pond and the trails of this park were my first, and very early, introduction to exploring, fishing, paddling, and hiking. Its very close proximity to where I grew up, and its easy access were what initially created my deep desire to explore, paddle, and hike as much as I do. I grew up in a time when we were eager to get outside and explore; cell phones and other electronic devices were not yet a part of my life.

I've hiked at this location far more than I've paddled Ross Pond. The view from the top of Ross Cliffs is spectacular because, under the cover of foliage, the tree top view goes on and on like there is no end. I always feel as though I'm far away from it all, when indeed it is all an illusion. The slight sound of highway traffic, which is louder on some of the paths, is a reminder of how close it all is beyond the thinly veiled tree cover.

As a child, Ross Pond seemed huge and inviting; as an adult, it looks like a typical sit-in-spin; however, there is a small inlet area and a tunnel under the highway bridge in the back left area of the pond. There are beaver huts, ducks, and other water birds beyond the tunnel-- sometimes an occasional muskrat can be seen. I was told by a friend that one of their friends once saw a bear back there!

I hike in this park once a year. This is a tradition that was started by my son and is continued in memory of his love for adventure and this hike in particular. I've missed a year here and there; however, it is usually an annual event shared with family, friends, and of course, our dogs. Be careful hiking to the top; there have been casualties on those cliffs over the years. Stay back from the edge and use caution around crevices, loose rocks, and steep inclines!

I would recommend Ross Pond for fishing or perhaps for a one-time fall paddle when the leaves have changed color--be sure to explore beyond the tunnel.

NOTES:

Five Mile River (Dayville to Danielson)
(See page 67)

SALMON RIVER

EAST HADDAM, CT

The Salmon River is a beautiful paddle and a river well known for its trout and salmon fishing....and I would like to add to that, it's many swans! We counted 50 swans at one location during our most recent paddle! This section of the Salmon River is typically an easy paddle up to the Leesville Dam and back.

TYPE: River

LAUNCH INFO:

This DEEP launch is located at the mouth of the river where it flows into the Connecticut River, and off E. Haddam Moodus Road (Rte 149) in East Haddam, CT. This launch can be used to access the Connecticut River or the Salmon River. When leaving the ramp, paddle right, and then immediately stay right to enter the Salmon River (staying left after paddling right from the ramp will take paddlers up the CT River). Paddling left from the ramp towards the bridge will take paddlers down the Connecticut River.

This is a formal launch intended for launching larger boats and has a large dirt parking area to support it. We easily launched to the left of the main launch to avoid disrupting the larger boats entering and exiting from the main launch. There are seasonal chemical toilets at this site.

LAST PADDLED: 9/27/15

POINT OF INTEREST:

You don't have to go all the way to Vermont to see a covered bridge. There is one that crosses the Salmon River; <u>it is not in this paddling area of this river</u>; but, it is close by and accessible through one of the walking trails found throughout the surrounding Salmon River State Forest. The covered bridge was built in 1840 and is called the Comstock Bridge. It is located in East Haddam, CT.

OUR EXPERIENCES:

Recently, we joined CT Shoreline Paddlers for a paddle up the Salmon River for a "Dam Jam" at the Leesville Dam.

What is a "Dam Jam?" Well, members of the CT Shoreline Paddlers showed me that it's a place to relax, paddle, have fun, enjoy music, and meet new people. Ten of us paddled to the Leesville Dam on the Salmon River, had lunch, and then relaxed on the grass and created music on one of the last really warm afternoons of the paddling season...light songs, even silly songs...a guitar, harmonica, shakers, clapping hands, kazoos, and maracas...oh yes, and a horn blast at the end of every song! Yes, it was as fun as it seems!

This fun approach to paddling is a gentle reminder that paddling can be taken to the next level without that next level involving speed and rapids! This fun-loving group of paddlers can be found online: CT Shoreline Paddling Adventures FB group.

NOTES:

SELDEN NECK STATE PARK ISLAND

CONNECTICUT RIVER BASE CAMPS!

LYME, CT

Selden Neck State Park Island is a wildlife preserve located on the Connecticut River, and only accessible by boat. It has 4 campsites for use by river paddlers. PRIOR RESERVATIONS ARE REQUIRED and there is currently a $5/person fee. Campers are only allowed to stay one night as these campsites are meant to assist paddlers passing by the island during river paddles. There are well-maintained out houses, picnic tables, and a fire pit with a grill top at each campsite. Awesome river paddle/campout experience for only $5/person! No dogs allowed. See DEEP reference top of page 192 for information regarding reservations..

TYPE: Four camp sites on Selden Island, Connecticut River

LAUNCH INFO:

These island camp sites can be accessed by boat from northern Connecticut River put-ins. Paddlers who would like to use the campsites for a one night stop over during a river paddle, can check out the camp sites prior to their trip by paddling across the river to the island from Castle Marina. As of the writing of this book, there is a minimal fee to launch and an additional fee to leave a vehicle at the marina over night.

The 4 base camps on Selden Neck Island:

CAMPSITE 1: Cedar Camp Area

We visited all the campsites except this one. It is located at the northern end of the island and not directly facing the open river. According to DEEP: max capacity is 20 campers.

CAMPSITE 2: Hogback Camp Area *(See photo page 192)*

This was our favorite of the three campsites that we visited. We immediately wanted to book this one as soon as we arrived, even though we had not yet seen the others! This site is up higher than the shoreline so it offers a better view and is not as obstructed by trees as was the Quarry Knob Camp Area. It doesn't have a low tide beach front like Spring Ledge; but, it has an inviting feel to it!

There is a small hill to climb (about 4 upward climbing steps); but, the view is worth it; we found it was easier to go up on the left when facing the site. Careful, the rocks at the water's edge are slippery. Site is open and has 2 picnic tables, clean outhouse with T Paper, and a large grill fire pit. According to DEEP: max capacity is 6 campers. Site is marked and identified with a sign.

Note: We returned to Selden Island on 8/26/15 and camped at this location. Beautiful spot! I even enjoyed an eagle lingering by the shore in the early morning hours while I sipped coffee by the fire!

CAMPSITE 3: Spring Ledge Camp Area

Tide permitting, Spring Ledge has a nice sandy beach area; but overall it did not appeal to us as much as Hogback. It had a fire pit grill, two picnic tables, clean outhouse with T Paper like the others, and it also had an additional sitting area. According to DEEP, max capacity is 8 campers. Site is marked and identified with a sign--also a large more predominant stick which may or may not still be there later on.

CAMPSITE 4: Quarry Knob Camp Area

This was our least favorite of the 3 campsites that we visited on the island. It offers more privacy than the other two that we visited; however, that privacy is offset by having a more obstructed view of the river than 2 and 3, and it's a longer walk to the campsite from the designated launch for this location. We paddled down river past the campsite, which is somewhat visible from the river, to the designated launch a short distance away, got out, and walked the path back to the campsite.

Paddlers will also have to walk the path to the launch area to use the outhouse because it's located at the launch. This site has more tree coverage, and while it offers more shade, it might expose campers to more ticks as well? It's important to note that, according to DEEP, this campsite is allowed 12 campers. Site is marked with a sign at the boat launch and the outhouse is there as well.

OUR EXPERIENCES:

We initially paddled over to the island from Castle Marina on two occasions to check out the island and camp sites. We returned for our campout/paddle on 8/25/15. During this paddling trip we explored down river locations that we hadn't previously explored, such as Brockway Island *(Page 47)* and Hamburg Cove *(Page 91)*. I highly recommend camping at this location during your down river paddles and explorations on the CT River. We enjoyed it very much!

Online reference: http://www.seldenisland.org/

Selden Neck State Park Island:
View from Hogback Campsite (*See page 190*)

SHETUCKET RIVER
BOAT LAUNCHES & PORTAGES

Caution: Paddling the Shetucket River should only be done by very experienced river paddlers who also possess prior knowledge regarding this river and its potential dangers! Paddlers who do not possess the above knowledge and skill level should not attempt to paddle this river unless they are accompanied by an experienced river paddler who is also familiar with paddling the entirety of this river. This is not a place for beginners!

Paddlers should wear a PFD and whistle at all times and realize and respect the potential dangers associated with this river! In addition to some of the more typical river challenges, the Shetucket River has additional dangers associated with functioning dams located on it. Stay back from ALL dams/falls and realize the functioning dams on this river can quickly and drastically change water levels in some areas! Paddlers who hear the warning blasts should immediately remove themselves and their gear from the water.

Paddle at your own risk and discretion; only you can determine what is, or is not, safe and appropriate for you and your level of experience and condition. It is your responsibility to determine the legality, suitability, and safety of paddling at the destinations and paddling routes in this book. Read all applicable signs at the launch sites, and be aware of boating regulations and potential dangers for each specific area before paddling. The author assumes no liability for accidents happening to, and/or injuries and/or damages sustained by readers and/or others who engage in the activities in this book. This book is for informational purposes only and should not be a paddlers only source of information regarding these paddling destinations.

Willimantic, CT: Philip "Lauter Park"

This launch is on the Natchaug River; however, this river quickly flows into the Shetucket River about 1 mile south of this location where the Natchaug River meets the Willimantic River to form the start of the Shetucket River. To paddle the entirety of the Shetucket River, this is the place to start. It is located on Jackson Street in Willimantic, CT. It is a nice easy sloping beach/launch area. (Rapids above this launch.)

Windham, CT: Recreation Park

"Rec Park" is located on Plains Road in Windham, CT. **Note:** I have never used this launch.

South Windham, CT: Route 203 crossing

The river may, or may not, be accessible at the Route 203 bridge in South Windham. I have used this area in the distant past; however, it has since been blocked off with large boulders, leaving a one car pull-off area and limited access. There is a steep incline and may not be suitable or safe for all paddlers. Scout before considering this potential point of entry/exit. *Not a formal launch.

Sprague, CT: Scotland Dam

Caution this is a functioning hydro-electric dam/plant that sometimes holds back and releases significant amounts of water; a horn will blast to warn paddlers to get themselves, their equipment, and kayaks out of the rising water until the water levels out again.

Note: The town of Sprague has, in the past, sponsored river paddles at this location by supplying transport for paddlers and their kayaks from the end point in Baltic back to the Scotland Dam on various scheduled days throughout the summer. These paddles were scheduled around the dam releasing the necessary water to do these trips.

Portage:

From the spillway side of the dam, the portage area will be river right at the end of the marker buoys. Portaging requires maneuvering up a slight hill and down a longer hill on the opposite side of the dam to a rocky launch area. These rocks can be slippery when wet.

On the falls side of the dam, the portage area is to the left when facing the dam. Paddlers approaching from this side, might not immediately see it because tall grass and foliage may initially block it from view. This option requires maneuvering up a semi-steep hill with kayaks.

Informal launch:

Many people fish the section of river that runs adjacent to Station Road near the dam. There are a few paths that lead across the active railroad tracks and to the water in this area. The path closest to the dam before going up the hill is the one with the least amount of hill going over the tracks. I've dollied and carried kayaks over these paths; paddlers choosing this option and who also own a dolly, should consider using it.

I have also launched by walking my kayak a very short distance through the brook by the bridge; however, I usually end up wet so I don't use that brook unless I'm wearing dry pants or it's a hot summer day. The river views in the immediate area of the dam are peaceful and I enjoy paddling in this area.

Baltic, CT: Salt Rock State Forest

* Camping available at this site

Salt Rock State Forest (DEEP site with camping) is located on 173 Scotland Road (Route 97) in Baltic, CT. Stay right after entering the park and follow "fishing" signs. It's a bit of a walk to the water from the parking area so I would advise using a kayak dolly for transport. The path to the water includes walking through a tunnel under the railroad tracks.

Temporary changes in water level occur in this area due to the demand and release of water from the Scotland Dam . The Scotland Dam is upriver and is a functional hydroelectric dam; due to varying demands of power they release or hold back water. Some paddlers might be in for a surprise if they decide to launch up river or from this location based on seeing additional water being released from the dam. Sometimes the river in this area looks nice and high, then the dam stops releasing water and paddlers find themselves pulling or carrying their kayaks! Timing can be everything on this river. I have pulled my kayak along behind me in less than knee deep water on this river more than once!

Baltic, CT: River Park

River Park is located on N Main Street (Rte 97) in Baltic, CT; south of the Salt Rock launch area and also located in Baltic. Coming from the north on Route 97, it's on the right, just prior to where Lords Bridge/Route 97 crosses the river and Route 97 then intersects with Rte 207. After entering the park, paddlers should stay left and drive to the end of the gravel area to the launch site.

Water temporarily rises and lowers in this area due to the Scotland Dam. The Scotland Dam is up-river and is a functional hydroelectric dam; due to varying demands of power they release or hold back water. Same situation can occur here as with the previously discussed Baltic launch (see prior entry above); the water can look paddleable based on water released from the dam and become less accessible when the dam stops releasing water.

Occum, CT: Occum Dam

FOUR LAUNCH SITES: the Occum Dam area has four launches; some better than others. #4 being the easiest to use, but farther down this section of river and closer to the lower mill dam.

1. Occum Dam portage area: Road-side parking with additional Sunday parking restrictions and the steep hill are the only downsides for using this portage area as a launch site. I have used this portage area to launch without problems. This area is located across from the church on Church Street in Occum, CT. This road is located near the Occum Dam. Scout before using this portage area as a launch site;

It may not be suitable entry for all paddlers, especially those with health conditions.

The portage area is outside the buoys to the left of the dam when paddling down river. It will be to the right of the falls when paddling up river; summer foliage sometimes blocks the falls side from view. I have portaged this dam paddling up river and I would not advise doing so if paddlers are not in top physical condition because the hill to be climbed with kayaks is long and steep! If paddlers are portaging to go down river, as most will, paddlers will be going down, not up, that hill.

2. Park (next to Occum Pizza on Route 97):

Seasonal chemical toilets

This park has a beautiful launch area to the right just a short distance after the parking area inside the park itself. The sign was slightly covered by trees during our last visit; however, if paddlers head towards the river from the parking lot and stay right, they can't miss it.

Paddlers will either have to dolly or carry their kayaks to the water because they can't drive up to it and unload. Beautiful easy launch once paddlers get to it. This launch area is very close to the Occum Dam and is the launch we used on our last visit to this area. This location also has seasonal chemical toilets at the end of the parking lot.

3. Commuter Parking Lot This very informal launch is on Route 97 at the Route 395 overpass. It would be "OK" for some more experienced paddlers to put in and take out. It's not a formal launch area; but, is more like a regularly used path to the water. Parking availability is based upon the use of the commuter lot adjacent to it. I would only use this as a last resort. This area is very close to the Occum Dam as well.

4. The Formal Boat Launch which includes a parking lot is located closer to the lower mill dam and is the launch that is farthest from the Occum Dam. Paddling right and up river from this location will bring paddlers to the Occum Dam/falls area.

DIRECTIONS: Continue from Occum Dam towards Norwich; after the mills, take a left onto Route 169 and take another left after the bridge (watch for boat launch signs). This is a formal launch with ample parking for car-top and trailers.

NOTE: *I do not know of an easy and safe way to portage the Ponemah Mill dam near this launch. Photo Ponemah Mill page 224.*

Norwich, CT: Greenville Dam

Caution this is a functioning hydro-electric dam/plant that sometimes releases significantly more water; a horn will blast to warn paddlers to get themselves and their equipment out of the water until the water levels out again. Paddlers should always wear an emergency whistle and PFD when paddling any part of the Shetucket River. Paddlers who do not have significant river paddling experience and prior experience paddling this river should not paddle on the Shetucket River unless accompanied by an experienced river guide who possesses extensive knowledge of this river and who has previously paddled it.

Portage:

When paddling down river, the portage area is river left just outside the buoyed area before the dam. It would be dangerous to attempt to paddle up river to this portage area due to the strong current and the possibility of addition water being released from this functioning dam.

The Greenville Dam launch/portage and access area is located at the intersection of Roosevelt, Smith, and Eighth Streets in Norwich, CT. At first glance, this might not look like a public access area from the street. It is surrounded by chain link fence and the area contains a small utility building and a small gravel parking area. If paddlers look closely at the fence, they will see the sign advising that this is a "public recreation area." *(See Greenville Dam page 85)*

If you like grinders and you're paddling in this area, consider visiting Vocatura (Italian) Bakery at 695 Boswell Ave (Route 12) in Norwich, CT. Fresh baked rolls. Best grinders in the area.

Howard T Brown Memorial Park

Howard T Brown Memorial Park is located at 100 Chelsea Harbor Dr. in Norwich, CT. Sometimes the parking area at this park is full due to activities going on in the area and paddlers will have to drop off, park, and walk back. There is a parking garage within sight of the park.

This launch will be on the right when paddling down the Shetucket River and is located at the convergence of the Yantic and Shetucket River with the Thames River. Shortly after passing under the railroad bridge (look for the railroad tunnel), paddlers will see the park on the right; following the park to the right, they will see the launch just after the pavilion. *(See page 101)*

NOTES:

DOG PADDLING TIP

Consider putting a bell on your dog's PFD. It's a lot easier to chase a loose dog through unfamiliar woods if the paddler can hear which direction the dog is going.

Hold the bell loosely as you walk around the store before purchasing it. You want one that will jingle with considerable movement, but not one that is going to become annoying by jingling every time the dog repositions itself in the kayak. A cheap Christmas bell (ornament) works well on Tiny's PFD.

I often share this information, and almost as often, I'm told that their dog is very obedient and would never take off. Never, is a big word with very little meaning in this situation. If the paddler's kayak flips and the dog is swept away and separated from them, the scared or even injured dog could be well on its way to some distant place before the paddler gets to shore. Safety precautions are not for the situations that we can predict and control; they are for the unexpected and the unforeseen!

For more information about kayaking with a dog, check out my book, DOG PADDLING WITH TINY: A Guide To Kayaking With A Dog at KayakingCTwithLou.com.

SWARMING OF THE SWALLOWS: CONNECTICUT RIVER

OLD LYME, CT

River paddlers who love paddling and birding, and who have never experienced the annual swarming of the swallows on the Connecticut River, should check this out! The fall swarming of the swallows at Goose Island is a unique event and not quite like any other paddling adventure. Imagine if you can, up to 500,000 swallows--that's probably difficult in and of itself! Now imagine separate swarms swooping down, pulling up, and blending with other swarms without mid-air collisions or mishaps--amazing!

It's not only entrancingly beautiful; but, also skillfully executed! I suggest arriving early and exploring the area before the swallows arrive at Goose Island. The actual event is over in minutes; so, arriving at least a little early will better ensure paddlers don't miss it.

This sunset event could be witnessed from the sandy beach on the northern tip of Calves Island; however, paddlers have the option of getting an even closer look by paddling up the Connecticut River side of Goose Island and watching the event from there. The latter option requires care and consideration of the other large and small boats embarking on the same adventure. This event is over at nightfall, so appropriate and adequate kayak lighting is necessary.

The swallows typically swarm in this area from mid August to October; however, too early or too late in the season could mean seeing less birds. Our September 19th visit was perfect!

This section of the Connecticut River is a tidal area and all tidal area precautions apply.

TYPE: Tidal River, Birding

LAUNCH INFO:

Pilgrim Landing is located on Pilgrim Landing Road in Old Lyme. It has about 8 parking spaces if everyone parks close together. This is an easy access site; however, it's not designed to accommodate trailers.

If the parking area at this site is full, the next closest launch is at Baldwin Bridge which is about a 1/2 hour paddle from Goose Island. Motor boats and larger boats can launch down river at Baldwin Bridge or up river at the Salmon River Launch which is located at the mouth of the Salmon River *(Page 187)*. For the more adventurous paddlers, this experience could be included in a down river paddle and even including an overnight stay at Selden Neck State Park Island *(See Selden Island entry page 189)*. This experience could be wrapped up with a bow in many different ways!

LAST PADDLED: 9/16/15

OUR EXPERIENCES:

We arrived in the afternoon and paddled in Lords Cove, later meeting up with our fellow paddlers on the sandy northern beach of Calves Island. From there, we paddled up the Connecticut River side of Goose Island, where we chose an area to hang out and wait.

The swarming of the swallows was a memorable event! Thousands of birds collected above Goose Island, forming funnel-like swarms that swooped down, floating gracefully across the sun drenched grasses; each swarm rolling upward towards the sky and folding in among thousands of other swallows doing the same! I became entranced within this aerial dance and lost track of time; when the night closed in around us, it was done! Just like that, the swallows were snuggled among the tall island grasses and ready for a peaceful sleep!

THAMES RIVER BOAT LAUNCHES

Howard Brown Memorial Park (Tidal area)

The Howard T Brown Memorial Park is located at 100 Chelsea Harbor Drive in Norwich, CT. Sometimes the parking area at this park is full due to activities going on in the area and paddlers will have to drop off, park, and walk back. There is a parking garage within sight of the park if the entire lot is full.

This launch is located within the Norwich Marina and at the convergence of the Shetucket and Yantic Rivers, creating the start of the Thames River. This launch can be used to paddle down the Thames River and up the Yantic and Shetucket Rivers; however, paddling up the Shetucket River will mean paddlers are paddling towards the functioning hydro-electric dam and the potential dangers involved in doing so.

Caution:

The Thames River is a tidal river, and also a short distance up river on the Shetucket River, is a functioning hydro-electric dam that holds back and releases water based on its needs. Both can affect the waters of the upper Thames River and very quickly change conditions. The right combinations of tide, wind, and release of water on the Shetucket River can sometimes create choppy water where the rivers come together near the park.

See page 85 for more details regarding conditions created by the Greenville Dam. Also see photo of the ship remains located on this section of the Thames River on page 217 and more details regarding this launch on page 101.

Poquetanuck Cove (Tidal area)

Poqutanuck Cove has a northern and southern launch. The southern launch is easily accessible at high and low tide; although, low tide will increase the distance walked to the parking lot with kayaks. The formal southern launch is on Route 12 a short distance from where the road crosses the cove in Preston/Gales Ferry, CT. It is a bit of a walk up hill to the parking area because boulders prevent paddlers from driving to the water; but, it is otherwise a nice launch *(See Poquetanuck Cove page 149)*.

CAUTION: Paddlers should watch for slippery semi-exposed rocks and larger boulders near the surface as they approach the Route 2A bridge and Poquetanuck Cove on the Thames River. At some lower water levels, it can be easy to slide up onto the side of one of these slippery boulders in the outer 1/3 of the river, creating a precarious situation.

Gold Star Memorial Bridge (Tidal area)

This launch is located under the Gold Star Bridge on State Pier Road in New London. It is accessible year round, has several parking spaces, and it is a DEEP site. It can be used as a take-out from northern launches or as a put-in for coastal access.

The affects of the tide can be felt a lot more in this lower part of the river than further north and paddlers should expect more and bigger boats. It is imperative that paddlers know the boating regulations and customary boating etiquette for this area and abide by them. Not suitable for beginners.

NOTES:

VERSAILLES POND

SPRAGUE, CT

Even though I live in the area, I have not visited Versailles Pond or nearby Papermill Pond in Sprague CT due to the mercury and PCB issues in Versailles and Papermill Pond. These two small ponds are connected by a waterway and Papermill Pond is about a ½ mile up Little River from Versailles Pond.

A July 2010 report from the CT Department of Health states that the major concern at Versailles Pond, at that time, was the contaminant levels found in sediment located in the middle of the pond beneath the water. It stated that "contaminant levels in the pond water and river water are very low." (1)

However, in that same year, the Norwich Bulletin published an article in which a state department of health toxicologist was quoted as saying, "Soil tests showed PCB levels ranged from between 12 and 150 times the normal level at select locations around the pond." (2). As of the publication date of this book, the online Connecticut Angler's Guide (DEEP) also lists a do not eat restriction on fish caught at Papermill and Versailles Pond and the connecting section of river in between due to high levels of **PCB and mercury** found in Versailles Pond. (3) Check for online updates because as time goes on these conditions may improve.

I'm not telling paddlers to not paddle or to paddle at this location. It's up to each paddler to assess the situation and decide what is and isn't safe and appropriate for them. I have provided some online links so that paddlers may become better informed about this site.

Several waterways have tested positive for PCBs, including my favored Quinebaug River (3); however, Versailles Pond is at the source of the **mercury and PCB** contamination for that pond and the immediate area around it.

References:

1.
http://www.ct.gov/dph/lib/dph/environmental_health/eoha/atsdr/versaillespondfactsheet.pdf

2.
http://www.norwichbulletin.com/article/20100730/News/307309896

3.
http://www.eregulations.com/connecticut/fishing/consumption-advisory/

NOTES:

WEST THOMPSON LAKE & QUINEBAUG RIVER PADDLE

THOMPSON, CT

The West Thompson Lake boat launch can be used to paddle around the lake or as a take-out for a down river paddle from the Fabyan Road launch or the Dudley (MA) launch on the Quinebaug River *(Also see page 159)*. Paddling for a short distance up river from West Thompson Lake or down river to this launch is dependent upon a favorable current and water level.

This section of river between the Fabyan Road Dam and West Thompson Lake is generally swift moving; I have experienced riffles, runs, and pools. Paddlers will maneuver turns in the river which exist within swift current and riffles, as well as some minor rock dodging. Later in the season, the water can be so low that paddlers bottom out in some areas and rock dodging can become more of an issue. The current will be slower and less challenging later in the season as well.

The section of river between the Brickyard Road Bridge and the next bridge is the half-way mark for a down river paddle from the Fabyan Dam launch. Paddlers will enter West Thompson Lake shortly after passing the remains of an old stone bridge on either side of the river. Paddling from the Fabyan Dam launch to West Thompson Lake takes about 2 1/4 - 3 hours, depending upon the water level and current. West Thompson Lake Park also has seasonal camping, toilets, picnic areas, benches, and hiking on marked trails.

TYPE: River Access, Lake, Camping, Hiking

LAST PADDLED: 4/13/16

LAUNCH INFO:

Put-in for a down river paddle to this location: This formal launch and parking area is located beside the bridge near the Fabyan Dam on Fabyan Road in (Fabyan) Thompson, CT. **Caution:** Signs state water does not meet health requirements for swimming and wading.

Note: I have launched from the Brickyard Road Bridge. It will take 1 - 1 ½ hours to paddle from this bridge to the Lake. There is no formal launch; however, it is not difficult to launch there. I recommend walking a little further into the woods where there is a better spot to launch.

Take-out: The West Thompson Lake boat launch is located on Campground Drive off Reardon Road in Thompson, CT. Watch for signs on Reardon Road. There are seasonal toilets, camping and picnic areas, hiking trails, benches, and a large parking & turning area.

Camping: http://www.recreation.gov/

OUR EXPERIENCES:

As is usually the case, we paddled down river to West Thompson Lake and then paddled around the lake. The water in this section of the river has sections of swift current and riffles. The current lessens as paddlers approach the lake. **Caution:** These conditions may increase and become more significant at higher water levels.

It is not the best place for spring wildlife and bird watching due to the swift current and riffles that we experienced during our recent spring paddle. There are sections that require paddlers to pay attention to the river and not the wildlife. A fellow paddler almost spun out at one sharp bend in the river. Great place for mid-late season wildlife and bird watching due to the slower current if the water level isn't too low. We did see litter and even a half submerged shopping cart. After entering the lake, we were joined by another paddler and ate lunch on one of the lake's sandy beach areas before continuing our paddle around the lake.

WHEELER POND

MONTVILLE, CT

Wheeler Pond is small and known by locals for bass fishing; however, it also should be considered by paddlers interested in bird watching. The swamp *(far left of the launch area)* and the area of Lilly Pads in front of it is a haven for birds.

The shoreline is sparsely populated with about a dozen homes, some jarringly visible and others sitting back partially out of sight and blending in with their surroundings. Traffic can be heard at some level in the background so there is no illusion of being away from it all. Bird watching and fishing would be my only recommendations for this pond.

TYPE: Pond, Bass Fishing, Bird Watching

LAUNCH INFO:

The unofficial launch area is located on Route 163 in Montville, CT. This pond and launch area will be found on the right side of Route 163 when arriving from Route 395. Watch for the launch just after the fire department pump set up and between the separation in the metal guard rails. Parking is tight and limited to 2 untrailered vehicles parked road side in front of, and ahead of, the launch area path.

LAST PADDLED: 7/2/14

OUR EXPERIENCES:

We paddled around the entire pond and then spent hours exploring the swamp and lily pad covered areas looking for birds and wildlife. We saw a few different breeds of duck, red wing black birds, heron, a pair of cormorants, hawks, swallows, and a few other large and small birds we could not identify. One small bird (not a swallow) literally hovered over the pads/water, seemingly unafraid beside our still kayaks, picking several bugs one at a time from the surface for several minutes. This bird was so close, I could have reached out and touched it with my paddle! Birds seemed, for the most part, to be unafraid; the secret being to paddle in stealth mode and occasionally sit quietly and patiently wait.

Two fishermen, who told us they frequent this pond, said that they caught 2 nice bass and were returning to give it another go..

I wouldn't suggest traveling to visit this site; however, paddlers who are in the area and who are into bass fishing or bird watching, might find it to be a worthwhile paddle.

NOTES:

WILLIAMS LAKE

LEBANON, CT

This lake is known for bass fishing; however, it might also be of interest to bird watchers. Birders and wildlife watchers can expect to see herons, king fishers, cormorants, varieties of ducks, geese, muskrat, and deer in the back portion of the lake where there are some inlet areas *(see our experiences below)*. There is also a campground located on the shore of this lake.

TYPE: Lake, Camping, Fishing, Bird/Wildlife Watching

LAUNCH INFO:

The Williams Pond boat launch is located within a small parking lot next to the dam on Route 207 in Lebanon, CT. Carry-in only; no trailer access to the water. The short path to the launch area is located to the left of the park sign at the separation in the guide rail.

Camping: Lake Williams Campground is located at 1472 Exeter Road (Route 207) in Lebanon, CT. For more information, check out http://lakewilliamscampground.net/

LAST PADDLED: 9/18/14

OUR EXPERIENCES:

I paddled casually around this 250+ acre lake with my dog on deck, investigating some of the many islands, and exploring the more swamp like areas towards the back of the pond. While we saw herons and cormorants in the main body of water, we saw most of the wildlife in a swampier area to the right back of the pond; in a river-like extension off the main body of water, I saw, herons, king fishers, cormorants, 2 varieties of ducks, geese, and muskrat.

I've been told by a few people that there are good size bass and pickerel to be caught in the back section of this pond near all those lily pads! I did often see fish swirls and a couple of times saw fish jump in that area of the pond as we paddled through it. This area is not completely covered in pads, but has groupings of pads with spaces of open water in between. However, there were enough pads to cause my dog, Tiny, to think that it might be a good idea to get out and walk on them! LOL! Tiny doesn't know it; but, he's lucky I stopped him.

There were two kayaks and one speed boat out on the lake while we were there. We visited on a weekday afternoon from about 3:30 PM until sunset. This is an enjoyable lake paddle with a variety of things to see if paddlers are interested in fishing and/or wildlife and birding.

NOTES:

INDEX

Paddle at your own risk and discretion; only you can determine what is, or is not, safe and appropriate for you and your level of experience and condition. It is your responsibility to determine the legality, suitability, and safety of paddling at the destinations and paddling routes in this book. Read all applicable signs at the launch sites and be aware of boating regulations for each specific area before paddling. The author assumes no liability for accidents happening to, and/or injuries and/or damages sustained by readers, and/or others, who engage in the activities in this book.

This book contains facts and also the opinions of the author who has paddled at each paddling destination in this book, unless otherwise stated. The opinions expressed in this book are those of the author and may not represent the opinion of others who may be mentioned in this book. It is a reference book for informational purposes only and should not be a paddler's only source of information for sites being paddled.

ALPHABETICAL INDEX
FOLLOWED BY TOWN INDEX

Ship wreck on the Thames River
See Howard Brown Memorial Park page 101.

INDEX BY TOWN

Paddle at your own risk and discretion; only you can determine what is, or is not, safe and appropriate for you and your level of experience and condition. It is your responsibility to determine the legality, suitability, and safety of paddling at the destinations and paddling routes in this book. Read all applicable signs at the launch sites and be aware of boating regulations for each specific area before paddling. The author assumes no liability for accidents happening to, and/or injuries and/or damages sustained by readers and/or others who engage in the activities in this book.

This book contains facts and also the opinions of the author who has paddled at each paddling destination in this book, unless otherwise stated. The opinions expressed in this book are those of the author and may not represent the opinion of others who may be mentioned in this book. It is a reference book for informational purposes only and should not be a paddler's only source of information for sites being paddled.

WOODSTOCK

RHODE ISLAND:

ASHAWAY
Potterville Dam/Pawcatuck River (CT/RI border)

CHARLESTOWN
Quonochontaug to Quonnie Beach (RI coastal)

PHOTO INDEX:

Shetucket River: Ponemah Mill, Norwich, CT
(South of the Occum Dam. See page 106)

Lou kayak sailing on Ninigret Salt Pond in Charlestown, RI

ABOUT THE AUTHOR

Lou Racine is a blogger and author of the book, DOG PADDLING WITH TINY: A Guide To Kayaking With A Dog. She has lived in Eastern Connecticut all her life and paddled extensively through out Eastern CT. Most recently, she has combined her love for writing, inspiring others, and paddling to create this book, Kayak Eastern Connecticut: 70 Eastern CT Paddling Destinations.

Rest assured, there will always be more to come, for Lou has a penchant for seeing and experiencing new places rather than re-experiencing the same again! Paddling year-round whenever temperatures permit, she is out the door at 40 degrees or above, searching for open water! During the traditional paddling season, she paddles one to three times a week, and coordinates river paddles and river paddle campouts.

Lou holds an Associate Degree with honors from Quinebaug Valley

Community Technical College in Danielson, CT. Preceding her son's fatal accident, she was working on her BS and actively involved in politics, and spent much of her spare time helping children. Her son's passing caused her to withdraw from community activities; however, she has started her journey back!

Lou is currently seeking to engage in collaborative efforts to inform and teach teens about the risks involved in kayaking, while at the same time, encouraging them to safely engage in this sport. She has taken the first step in an ongoing effort to help prevent paddling tragedies among inexperienced paddlers by placing significant emphasis on potential dangers while writing this book. For more information regarding how you may be able to assist her efforts, see Acknowledgements on page 5.

Currently, she lives on a farm in North Eastern Connecticut with her long-time inspiration, Cecil, and their two dogs, Tiny and Deacon. The two dogs can often be seen paddling with them during the warmer months of the year.

.OTHER BOOKS BY THIS AUTHOR

Dog Paddling With Tiny:
A GUIDE TO KAYAKING WITH A DOG

COMING SOON IN 2016

Kayak With A Dog
COLORING BOOK

Email: KayakingCTwithLou@paddlingCT.com
Please no solicitation

KayakingCTwithLou.com

Made in the USA
Middletown, DE
16 June 2020